COUNTRY LIFE BOOK OF

BRITAIN
THEN AND NOW

COUNTRY LIFE BOOK OF

BRITAIN
THEN AND NOW

A unique visual record of
Britain over the last 100 years

Edmund Swinglehurst

PYRAMID

The author wishes to thank Jane Robinson and
Elissa Swinglehurst for their help in researching
some of the information contained in this book.

To Nicholas

title page
Evesham, Worcester, 1890.

First published in 1988 by
The Octopus Publishing Group plc.
This edition published 1988
by Guild Publishing,
by arrangement with
The Octopus Publishing Group,
Michelin House, 81 Fulham Road,
London SW3 6RB

Printed in Spain

CN 9595

Contents

The Wishing Well, 1890. *The Victorian understanding of the countryside as a bucolic paradise is vividly expressed in this picture; in its day one of Francis Frith's bestsellers.*

Introduction

Shakespeare's birthplace, Stratford-on-Avon, c.1850 (below). *In the 1850s, Stratford-on-Avon was a sleepy little village deep in the Warwickshire countryside. Ten years later the railway arrived and Shakespeare's birthplace, which was a butchers shop, became the town's greatest tourist asset. Soon, the house was restored to its original plans – gables, porch and all. Today it is open to the public as the Shakespeare Trust's Museum.*

In the years after Queen Victoria ascended the throne, Louis Jacques Mande Daguerre, a Frenchman, and William Henry Fox Talbot, an Englishman, succeeded in producing a photographic image on plates coated with chemical compounds of silver. Their separate discoveries made possible, for the first time, an accurate visual recording of places and events, not one transformed by the imagination of artists. The new medium immediately attracted the attention of educated Victorians who recognised it as another of the great steps forward, which their age was making in the march towards human progress and enlightenment.

Rule Britannia!

In the 1860s Britain was well under way to becoming the world's greatest industrial nation but there were still many areas of the country where the old agricultural life-style continued. The rural economy was, however, deteriorating decade by decade, resulting in ever more people moving to the industrial cities where work, though often unpleasant, was available. The decay of rural areas was an inevitable consequence of industrialization.

Britain, finding itself the world's largest producer of manufactured articles and constantly seeking new markets overseas for its goods, came to believe in the principle of free trade between nations. This would enable Britain to sell its products to all over the world and, in return, the raw materials of those countries to be imported and turned into manufactured articles.

Free trade also meant that food would become more abundant and cheaper for the workers in the new industrial towns. The staple diet of the urban poor being bread, it was advantageous to import wheat from the great grain fields of the United States, which had been sown by the settlers after the prairie Indians had been driven off their hunting grounds. Suppliers from the vast granary of America lowered the price of wheat and the British farmer with his limited acres was unable to compete. Firstly, the small tenant farmers, of whom there had once been many, merged with the larger farms; then even the large farms found survival difficult, though the advent of farm machinery improved

Parliament Street, Harrogate, 1907. *Parliament Street, in the centre of the town, retains much of its old atmosphere. The Royal Baths and Assembly Rooms, opened in 1897 at the northern end of the Street, once the largest hydrotherapy establishment in Europe, no longer provide sulphur baths and hot poultices as they once did for rheumatic visitors. Today, Harrogate is a handsome resort town and conference centre.*

A drive in the country, Broughton, c.1920. The 1920s saw the introduction of the first really mass-produced motor cars which were inexpensive enough for the middle classes to discover the joys of the open road. In less than a generation the motor car changed every aspect of the British way of life.

and the importance of market towns consequently declined.

In an effort to maintain the flow of visitors who used to throng the towns, other ways of attracting the public had to be found. Some of the towns exploited the growing demand for leisure and entertainment among working people by enlarging the scope of their traditional fairs. Today the activity at fairs such as the Nottingham Goose Fair and the Warwick Mop Fair, bear little resemblance to their original purpose.

Civic pride

The main feature of the new industrial towns of late Victorian times were the civic centres which symbolized their affluence and aroused a strong sense of pride among the inhabitants. The idea of local government being able to represent the people was a relatively new one. A Local Government Act was passed in 1871 but it was Joseph Chamberlain, Mayor of Birmingham 1873-76, who laid down the actual principles of local government which are still valid. His belief that the role of a town's council was to provide for all the essential needs of the community was considered a very radical view but today, when housing, health, welfare and even leisure is the concern of local councils, it is taken for granted.

The enhanced role of local government awoke both in the governors and the governed a heightened sense of the importance of their locality and a desire to create worthy civic centres. The 1870s were therefore a period of extensive municipal building with magnificent town halls, council houses, museums, art galleries, libraries and other buildings in a rich variety of styles. Many of these edifices were inspired by the great masterpieces of architecture of the past; there are Roman temples, Renaissance mansions, Venetian palazzi and Gothic town halls surrounded by lesser buildings in the same eclectic styles.

What was wrong with the English architecture of Wren, Adam and Nash? The answer is, of course, that it lacked the necessary grandeur whereas the architecture of the successful city states of the European Renaissance, which were becoming increasingly familiar to the growing number of British travellers

the situation in one way by allowing the farmers to dispense with labourers. As farming declined, so did the crafts needed to maintain the work of the countryside, the craftsman-made utensils gradually being replaced by the factory-produced ones. In the 1880s the farriers were shoeing horses in workshops that would soon become garages, the haymakers would soon be replaced by combine harvesters.

The market towns had long been the centre of farming life, and in the market squares, animals in their rows of stalls or herds of sheep and cattle in the streets would stand patiently while the farmers talked business. But these towns were already changing by the 1880s. In the early Victorian period most people would visit their nearest market town to buy a year's supply of essential items of food: sacks of grain for making bread, flitches of ham, cheeses and anything else that would keep. The expansion of the railway systems, however, changed the habits of country people instilled over centuries for trains made it possible for farm products to be bought by large distributors who in turn supplied retail the shops. This enabled people to buy food at times other than market days,

Covent Garden, London 1890s. *Covent Garden started life as Convent Garden. In the 17th century, it was redesigned by Inigo Jones as an Italian style piazza, to house London's famous fruit and vegetable market. The market closed in 1974 to re-open in new quarters at Nine Elms near Vauxhall Bridge.*

Covent Garden, London, today. *Nowadays, Covent Garden leads a more gaudy life as a tourist centre with restaurants, cafés and boutiques and almost non-stop shows of street entertainers who perform where Bernard Shaw's Eliza Doolittle of 'Pygmalion' once sold flowers.*

abroad, possessed both the grand historical connections and the appropriate appearance for these new, powerful, local governments.

The visual impact of these Victorian civic buildings with their noble columns and soaring towers has, in many cases, been diminished by the more recent additions of contemporary multi-storied blocks. But even today they make a forceful image of a time of supreme self-confidence and power.

London

People still moved with a certain leisurely self-confidence among the horse-drawn vehicles in the streets of provincial towns in Victorian times. London, in contrast, was already a great metropolis, and also then one of the greatest ports in the world. Traffic jams are certainly not a recent phenomenon – hansom cabs and horse-drawn buses were frequently held up in the narrow, congested streets. In an attempt to improve road conditions, new thorough-fares were built along the Embankment and the Strand was widened. From the 1870s onwards much of London, too, was being extensively rebuilt. Its river was filled with ships from every part of the world, loading and unloading their cargoes at the new warehouses that lined the south bank of the Thames.

London was the centre of an Empire that was still growing steadily, creating more trade and incidentally involving itself in more military expeditions to Afghanistan, China, Uganda, British Honduras and other outposts, as well as encouraging more migrations of British peoples all over the world.

Education

Since most people were not able to read and write in the first half of Victoria's reign, few were aware of the events that were making Britain great but that began to change as education came to be recognized, though not universally, as a good thing. In 1870 a notable step forward was made by an Act making elementary education available to all. It was estimated that more than three million children were in need of education. Though good in intention, the Act did not immediately bring about an end to illiteracy for there were not enough schools to accommodate such numbers. Previously, schools had been run by local churches or founded by benefactors who had set up trusts for the poor of their locality. Throughout the 18th century these had been allowed to decay. Even the old-established grammar and public schools were often incapable of teaching any subjects other than Latin and Greek and unable to keep any kind of discipline. The ancient universities of Oxford and Cambridge were in Victorian times still places of privilege open only to those able to pay the fees and, indeed, with the right family background.

The general interest in education was fostered by the ideas of Samuel Smiles, who believed that achievement was a matter of people improving themselves. The growing urban population began to demand more adequate education for children destined for a competitive life in an industrial society, with the result that proprietary schools and technical institutes were created. Their example exerted some influence on education in general, but even so a secondary school education did not become universally available by law until 1937 when the school leaving age was raised to 15. This was not in fact implemented until World War II ended in 1945.

The cathedral towns also played an important part in the education of the administrators of the nation from the earliest years of Christianity. This church influence on education continued until the 19th century, interrupted in the 16th century by Henry VIII's Dissolution of the Monasteries, which caused a hiatus in the works of such schools until new charters were granted by royal consent.

A sense of heritage

The growth of travel and of literacy brought to the British people a sense of their heritage and history, which awoke an interest in old buildings. This enthusiasm was also fostered by the Romantic movement's pleasure in ancient, ivy-covered buildings, deserted towers and other relics of a chivalric age which feature frequently in the poems of such great romantic poets as Coleridge, Keats, Shelley and Wordsworth. The growing interest in Britain's history and the growth of a middle class who had the time and money, resulted in many people taking excursions to such places as Belvoir Castle and Alton Towers on Thomas Cook's tours, and reading the romantic historical novels of Sir Walter Scott and Robert Louis Stevenson.

An interesting comparison between the castles and abbeys, as they were in Victorian times and as we know them today, shows a very different approach to historical ruins. Then, they were ivy-covered and surrounded by brambles and other vegetation which gave them the appropriate air of romantic enchant-ment which was a particular hallmark the Romantic Movement; today these ruins have been denuded of their vegetation in the interests of preservation of the fabric of the buildings: look, for example, at Brambletye in Sussex and Berry Pomeroy Castle in Devon. Another big difference between the attitude to ancient buildings then and now is that, today, the ruins are seen to be material assets of the tourist industry and their conservation is as much a matter of self-interest as nostalgia for the past.

The leisure scene

Tourism, or rather leisure travel, was another profitable theme for Frith, as those who visit beauty spots or seaside resorts inevitably feel inclined to take away with them some souvenir which will revive memories of pleasant times. Frith's coverage of the leisure scene was comprehensive, including the buildings that were springing up in the resorts, the esplanades, piers, winter gardens and, of course, the scenes on the beach. But he did not neglect other places where late Victorians enjoyed the new freedom to travel and to enjoy leisure for its own sake; and he added to his collection photographs of the spas which were still popular with a section of the population, and the mountains and lakes which appealed to lovers of the open air.

Today, when the idea of travel and leisure is taken for granted, it is difficult to imagine the excitement and wonder which were aroused at first by being confronted with the grander aspects of nature in the form of mountains or the sea. In the latter part of Victoria's reign, such encounters by people who had known only the village or town where they were born were happening with increasing frequency; the feeling of amazement that people experienced was coupled with a sense of freedom that fired the will to search for a better life with more pleasure and less drudgery.

In the changes that have taken place between the 'then' of the Victorian Age and the 'now' of our era, perhaps the most fundamental are those relating to attitudes to work and leisure. No longer are we prepared to work 16 hours a day or to allow others, including children, to be the low-paid slaves of society; work is now seen to be a means to an end rather than the end in itself.

Before the Victorians, nobody questioned the purpose to which society was directed – today we question everything. This radical transformation of the individual and the society in which he lives is the product of the Victorian age with its conventionality and its radicalism, its self-interest and its altruism, and as one looks at the people in the old photographs, one cannot help wondering whether they would have approved of the 20th century which they created. □

Guildford, High Street, 1923. As the 20th century progressed so the motor car became the single most potent element for change in the country. People could travel far afield, easily and in comfort and industry could transport goods more effectively. But the price was roads and more roads, a carpet of tarmacadam and concrete.

Life in the Country

The small size of Britain compared to other industrial countries is perhaps the reason why the British people nurture a special passion for their countryside. This has been expressed in literature by writers like Thomas Hardy and Wordsworth, and in art by Constable, Turner and many others. In this chapter we look at the countryside, its villages and market towns. The fine detail tells the story of the change in country life during the past one hundred years; in them are scenes of the countryside and of the people, and of the regions unknown before the age of the motor car.

Milk collecting, Hindhead, Surrey, 1907. Before the age of the huge, motorized milk-container lorry (left), most milk was collected in individual metal churns from farm gates and taken to dairies and distribution depots. In 1907, milk was still carried about in pails, as the man in this picture is doing at Broom Squires Cottage, Hindhead. In order to balance the weight and to ease the load, the pails were chained to a yolk which was supported on the back.

When Queen Victoria came to the throne the British countryside was still largely unaffected by the Industrial Revolution, though the Agrarian Revolution that had begun in the reigns of her Hanoverian predecessors, was being felt by more and more of her subjects. Despite nearly half the population having moved into the new industrial towns by the 1840s, the urban influence which was to change attitudes in the country had not yet made much impact. The countryside, though altered in appearance in many parts of England by the considerable increase in 'enclosure' Acts in the reigns of George III and IV, was still very largely ruled by landed gentry and squirearchy who were a powerful force in rural society through their positions as employers and Justices of the Peace, and through their working alliance with the established church.

Many great landlords no longer lived in their country estates throughout the year, having acquired the habit of spending several months of each year in London, and even of travelling abroad. Nevertheless, their influence was apparent in every aspect of country life. It was they who provided land for their tenants and allotments for the distressed labourers, employed armies of country people's sons and daughters as servants, licensed craftsmen to carry on their trades and had a considerable say in the appointment of the local clergy and school-teachers.

Until conditions in the countryside began to worsen later in Victoria's reign, owing to the adoption of Free Trade principles, with the consequent importation of cheap food from abroad, especially America and the 'Colonies', few people questioned this way of life. But when desperate country people began to move into towns and absorb the democratic ideas which grew out of the large agglomerations of workers, very rapidly things began to change.

Threshing, Somerset, 1920s (left). *The steam traction engine changed life in the countryside, not only reducing manual labour but also diminishing the community spirit of the times when the whole village shared a seasonal task. This engine is doing the threshing and taking the corn stalks up an endless belt to the top of a growing hayrick. On the far side the tip of a ladder can be seen which was used by the men on to the rick to spread out the hay in an orderly manner and finish off the top.*

The grain is being gathered in the stacks behind the man on the right of the picture who appears anxious about the position of the post holding up the machine.

Harvesting, Somerset, c.1900 (right, above). *Everyone lent a hand with haymaking and the women spent hours and sometimes days gathering up any corn left by the reapers. This gleaning was vital to the poor farm labourers for it could yield a sack of corn which would be carefully conserved and turned into flour for making bread during the year. Since labourers were usually too poor to pay the local miller, he would keep a tenth of the milled flour for himself. Though it was hard and back-breaking work, the haymaking and the gleaning was usually a festive time for most country people. Today, with better standards of living for all, gleaning has become a forgotten occupation.*

Ploughing, Leatherhead, 1925 (right). *In the 19th century a more scientific approach to farming fostered by the Royal Agricultural Society, founded in 1889, led to the development of new tools for the farmer. Ploughs which had been originally made of wood had already been produced in cast-iron, but new models continued to be invented to cope more efficiently with different types of soil. The Norfolk plough was particularly suitable for the rich, soft soil of East Anglia. Its main characteristic was the long central beam resting on a gallows which transmitted its weight to a pair of wheels. This gave more control to the ploughman who could guide the plough with one hand and so proceed much faster.*

Haymaking, Netherbury, near Bridport, Devon, 1912 (above). *By the beginning of the 20th century the traditional system of tenant farming had begun to break down as large estates were sold to pay death duties. Farming methods remained much the same as in early Victorian times, however. Manual labour and horsepower were still the means by which farms were worked, as in this picture where two men with two horses are gathering together the crop in readiness for stacking it in sheaves.*

One thing that had changed was the style of dress of farming people. Instead of the leather gaiters and smock of earlier times, farmers had adopted a version of town dress: corduroy trousers, a waistcoat and a tweed or corduroy jacket.

Most farming folk were poor, receiving none of the subsidies or benefits that they do today, and farming communities were small, self-contained units whose social life revolved round the village, the public house and the church.

Today harvesting is a computer-controlled, thundering-machine kind of business. The crop is cut at the precise moisture content to facilitate drying in vast hot air driers. Contractors are hired with massive combine harvesters to cut, thresh and store the grain even in the middle of the night if that is the optimum time. These machines have enabled Britain to produce enough grain for all our needs and, sadly, to add to the ever-growing grain mountain of Europe and the ever-escalating loss of our patchwork countryside.

The idyll that was England

In the mid-19th century, the farming landscape of England was a patchwork of fields, the majority of roads were unpaved and narrow, and most villages were merely isolated groups of cottages with little contact with any urban community larger than the nearest market town. For most inhabitants of Britain, their knowledge of England, Scotland or Wales was limited to the few square miles within walking or riding distance of their homes. The village was the unit of rural life created at the time of open-field farming when houses were grouped together in the centre of the agricultural lands belonging to a particular land owner. He owned most of the houses in the village and leased them to his tenants and labourers so long as their employment lasted – a system which often brought great hardship to those who became too ill or too old to work, unless the landlord was a man who also endowed alms-houses in which those who depended on him could end their days.

Village life

Though there were many different levels to village life it was surprisingly homogenous with a great sense of interdependence among the inhabitants. Dominating village life were the people in the big house, the best of whom felt a paternal responsibility for the villagers, the ladies occupying themselves in their welfare, visiting the sick and providing employment for the poor, the elderly and the disabled. This good sense of communal responsibility still continues in many of the rural parts of Britain.

The villagers included many specialist craftsmen who kept the fabric of the agricultural community together, such as blacksmiths, wheelwrights, osiers, curriers, weavers, hedgemakers, bakers, cobblers and even rat-catchers and warreners, the latter

Smithy, Somerset, 1890 (above). *This picture looks as if it were specially posed for the occasion – probably because it needed a time exposure and if the workers had been moving, their image would have been blurred. The scene is, however, descriptive of a smithy of the period. The man on the right is bringing the fire up to the correct temperature to heat the metal by pumping the bellows with one hand while he pokes the coal with his fire irons. In the centre of the picture the smith holds a piece of hot metal for a horseshoe in the tongs while preparing to knock it into shape with the hammer. The boys with the sledge hammers look a bit de trop but they would have really been needed if the smith had been working on some larger piece of metal for perhaps a cart-wheel or axle. The old man looking at the camera seems to be suspicious of this new fangled idea; he probably started in the smithy before photography was invented.*

having a licence to snare rabbits in a number of warrens. At the hub of village life were the parson, the school-teacher, the doctor and the solicitor, though many villages had neither of the last two.

Country life in the mid-19th century was by no means idyllic. There were few of the comforts we take for granted now; there was no electricity, water had to be drawn from a well or collected from the village pump, draughty cottages were heated by small, smoky fires and there were no means of conserving fresh meat. Most people's diet was frugal, based on potatoes and root vegetables with an occasional piece of pork or mutton. Those who could manage it kept chickens or rabbits, and the pride of some families was their pig, which was spoiled and cosseted, as Flora Thompson describes in *Lark Rise to Candleford*, until it was ready to be killed, a ceremony which all the family would attend.

A life in the day

Daily life in a village was a humdrum affair by modern standards, with the length of the working day regulated by the rising and setting of the sun. Before dawn, many houses in a village would already be astir as the men prepared to go out into the fields or to groom the horses that would draw carts or help with the ploughing or other activities, and the children got ready for their often long walks to the nearest school. The men would be given their midday meal of bread and a slice off the flitch that hung by the stove, wrapped in a handkerchief.

The women busied themselves about the home, cleaning, patching, hoeing the vegetable garden and fetching water. Once a week they did the laundry in large pans of water heated over the cast-iron stove. If the weather was fine the laundry would be hung out in the open but when it rained it had to be suspended in the house, often for

Coopers, Somerset, 1890 (below). *The cooper's craft flourished in the 18th and 19th centuries when breweries increased the demand for barrels. As well as barrels coopers made butter churns, casks, tubs, buckets and small bever barrels in which farm labourers carried ale or cider for their midday meal. Though many of the coopers became large businesses, some local village coopers continued in business until after World War II when the products of their craft became largely factory-made in plastic or in metal.*

In this picture the three men are at work on different stages of barrel-making, the one in the centre is cutting staves to an appropriate length and thickness while the one on the right is backing them, curving the outer side of them, with a long knife, leaning the wood on a 'horse' for support. On the left the third man is preparing the hoops that will fit over the barrels, the staves of which have to be carefully jointed to ensure a tight fit. The hoops would be heated then hammered tight over the staves so that when the iron cooled the shrinkage in the metal would pull the wood firmly together. A cooper's workmanship was very precise and the combination of handcrafted wood and hammered iron had a beauty that modern plastic and metal products can never possess.

Basket-makers, Somerset, 1890 (left). There was plenty of employment for basket-makers in the 19th century for they not only made baskets but also furniture and cages and traps of various kinds. They used willow which was either stripped, as the man on the left of the picture is doing, to produce white osiers, or left with the bark on, like the ones used in the eel and fish traps on the right. In this busy scene the workers come from all age groups of the community, including children who were luckier than those who worked long hours as chimney sweeps or in coal mines. There is an unusual preponderance of women workers who perhaps were freer to take on the piece-work which this cottage industry offered.

Eventually, this industry succumbed, like many other crafts, to the march of progress and as time went on more and more basketwork was made in factories by machine, later to be supplanted by the plastic replica.

Fishermen, Bucks Mills, Devon, 1906 (right). Along the rugged north coast of Devon, fishermen built their tiny villages in the ravines that cleave the cliffs. One of these, reached by a long, narrow road down a wooded valley, is Bucks Mills, teetering on the edge of a precipitous slope. A path where fishing boats used to be left out of reach of stormy seas, still leads from the village to the rocky shore below. Donkeys were once used for transporting the nets and other fishing gear from village to shore, and were harnessed with wooden saddles whose width was increased by straw-filled sacks to prevent the nets dragging.

The close-knit community of Bucks Mills kept very much to themselves; because of their dark hair and swarthy faces they were believed to be descendants of a wrecked ship of the Spanish Armada.

Today, Bucks Mills, unlike its neighbour Clovelly, retains much of its old atmosphere because there is little space for car parking.

The village pub

The village public house is a lovable British institution dating back to the middle ages and derived from the 'inn' or 'tavern'. Almost every village had its beer house which was in many cases just a cottage where the village men would come and drink served by the lady of the house or her daughters. Invariably the man of the house would work locally. Many pubs would brew their own beer and some developed into large brewing concerns. Henry Thrale, a benefactor of Samuel Johnson owned a large and prosperous brewery in the 1750s in south London which supplied the local area.

The pub was an important social centre for the village and would be used for gatherings, as a centre for sport and recreation. They were also the place in the village where jobs might be advertised by word of mouth, and the place where village matters would be discussed and organised.

The Barley Mow Inn Clifton Hampden, Oxfordshire, 1890 (above and left). *The Barley Mow Inn today looks very much as it did when Jerome K. Jerome chose it as one of the places visited by the* Three Men in a Boat, *but since this picture was taken a road has been built across the space where the man and the horse are standing, thus allowing cars to disturb the peace of those enjoying a quiet glass of ale at the trestle tables. Behind the thatched pub there is now an unobtrusive house and by the gate on the near side of the road a pub sign swings in the breeze.*

Clifton Hampden village, which is on the other side of a narrow bridge surrounded by trees, has managed to preserve a rural air. Besides the splendid thatched pub, the village possesses such essentials of English villages as a fine church, St Michael and All Saints, and a small village shop which caters to residents' needs as well as providing freshly-made ham rolls for visitors.

Speldhurst, near Tunbridge Wells, Kent c.1900 (above). *The pubs and the church are never far from each other in English villages and the congregation from one place often ends up at the other. In this photograph, a patient horse delivering barrels of beer waits for his driver who may be talking business over a 'jar' with the publican or even perhaps visiting the vicar!*

The Jolly Farmer, Farnham, Surrey, 1904 (above and right). *By the turn of the century rural public houses were places of recreation as well as alcoholic drinks, far removed from the 'gin palaces' of the big cities. Class divisions existed in the various bars and ladies rarely entered, except when accompanied by a gentleman who would take them to the saloon or lounge bar. The public bar was used by labourers who could test their skills at such popular pastimes as darts, table skittles and shove-halfpenny.*

The Jolly Farmer in Bridge Square was a popular pub in what was, in 1904, rural Surrey. William Cobbett, whose Rural Rides *recorded the decay of the English countryside as early as the 1830s, was born in the pub, now renamed after him, in 1762. Other relics of a rich past still surviving in modern Farnham, include the keep and tower of a castle, and Vernon House, now the town library, where Charles I is reputed to have stayed.*

several days, until it dried.

The women might make a trip to the village shop, then a humble affair with a few of the essentials of life; some of them still exist, though now stocked with the products of national manufacturers. The shop was also the village meeting place and a good source of gossip.

The main meal of the day was eaten on the men's return from work. It was usually known as 'tea' and might consist of a slice of bacon, vegetables and bread. Sometimes the diet was supplemented by small birds such as sparrows, thrushes and blackbirds caught by the children of the family in nets; more rarely the father of the family might go out and poach a rabbit or hare.

Larger villages would boast an inn, where the men would gather after tea, discussing the affairs of the village or playing games like shove-halfpenny or darts. Later in the evening they would perhaps join in a sing-song round the piano.

The character of the village

The distinctive character and appearance of country villages were markedly different in one part of Britain from another. Geology played an important part in shaping local architecture. In lowland areas with plenty of agricultural land and woodland – East Anglia and the Midlands, for instance – houses tended to be built of timber and to have thatched roofs. Along the edges of the chalk hills of southern England and the Home Counties flint was used extensively, with the mortar needed to hold the roughly-shaped flint together coming from the lime in the chalk. Often the flint was combined with bricks, particularly in areas such as Buckinghamshire where the chalk and clay were found together. There were also the villages of stone houses which have a particular appeal to us today, especially those in the Cotswolds where the stone has a warm, glowing quality. Stone was and, of

Bidford on Avon, Broom, Warwickshire, 1910 (above). *Bidford and Broom are two of the eight villages mentioned in the old rhyme, attributed to William Shakespeare, which runs 'Piping, Pebworth, Dancing Marston, Haunted Hillborough, Hungry Grafton, Dodging Exhall, Papist Wexford, Beggarly Broom and Drunken Bidford'. Whether or not the last two villages deserved the calumny is not recorded, but it was at Bidford that Shakespeare caroused one night with his companions at the Falcon Inn and slept off the effects under a tree.*

The cottage architecture is traditional. The timbered frame of the houses was filled in with twigs and mud, known as wattle and daub, and the straw thatching came from wheat, straw or from reeds which would probably have been transported from Norfolk.

Old Ford Farm, Bideford, Devon, 1870s (right). *For many, life on a farm was hard. Farms supported sizeable families, each member of which was assigned special tasks. Everyone worked from dawn to dusk. In summer it was no doubt hot and smelly and in winter freezing cold. But at least they did not have to suffer the drudgery of factory work. There were few amenities in their homes: this picturesque-looking, stone farm cottage lacked running water, sewage and electricity. The chickens in the cobbled courtyard wandered freely in and out of the house no doubt with the childrens pet dog and any cats that were around and often the cobbles were deep in cow dung and refuse. The forked branch in the centre of the yard held up the clothes-line, and the building on the right of the house was probably a pigsty or cowshed.*

Alfriston, Sussex, 1895 and 1921 (left). *The Saxons were the first inhabitants of Britain to establish farming communities; one such was at Alfriston in the Cuckmere valley in East Sussex. The little village still has a rural atmosphere and many of its well-preserved houses date back to medieval times. One of these is the Clergy House which stands near St Andrew's church on the village green, known as the Tye. In 1895 the house was in a sad state, as can be seen in the first photograph, but the newly formed National Trust came to the rescue, acquired it and began to restore it to its original appearance. The second photograph shows the house in 1921 after its restoration with its new roof and cottage garden. The timber frame, made from trees from the forests that stretched across southern England, and the thatch, made from the stalks of the grain crops, were also carefully restored. Today, the house gives visitors an opportunity to examine a typical dwelling of a 15th-century countryman.*

Castle Combe, Wiltshire, 1907 (right). *Hats were worn by everyone, even in country villages, in the years before World War I and they add a colourful note to this scene at Castle Combe. This village, regarded by most people as the quintessence of an English country village, has changed very little over eighty years. The houses are built of Cotswold stone, with steeply pitched roofs designed to allow the rain to run off rapidly. The stone bridge over the Bybrook was a good place for a quiet gossip in 1907, as was the small, covered market seen at the top of the street. Castle Combe was a wool village and, like many Cotswold villages, has a fine church, St Andrew's (just out of sight to the left of the picture), built with funds provided by the merchants whose wealth came from flocks of sheep that pastured in the surrounding hills.*

The Manor House, first built in the 14th century, was destroyed and rebuilt, though some traces of the original building remain in what is now an attractive country house hotel.

course, still is also used in village architecture in many parts of the country including Cornwall, Wales, the Lake District and the Pennines.

The end of the era

By late Victorian times, many villages had already begun to decay, particularly in the south, the area most hard hit by the workings of Free Trade. To industrial Britain, Free Trade seemed a sensible policy for a nation that was outstripping all its Continental rivals as a manufacturer of everything from Macclesfield ties to Middlesbrough engines. Britain ruled the seas and over a third of the world's merchant fleets were British. Britain's factories needed the world's raw materials and the world needed Britain's manufactured products. Moreover, much of the world was being filled with British people, especially the 'new' lands of Australia, New Zealand and Canada. Dazzled by the prospects ahead, British governments sacrificed the English countryside to William Blake's dark satanic mills.

Like the Repeal of the Corn Laws which some had seen as a blow to British agriculture, Free Trade did not have an immediate deleterious effect on rural life. The wheat fields of America which were to pour their produce into Britain at the end of the century had not yet been sown. In fact, much of the northern countryside benefited from Free Trade in the first decades of the 19th century for the increase in industrial activity and the growth of the large urban centres created a greater demand for farm produce.

More and more of the rural population, seduced by the promise of an easier life in the towns, began to desert the country. As time went on the inventiveness of industry introduced the country people to products hitherto made by local craftsmen but now available much more cheaply from noisy, machine-filled factories.

The dawn of the new age

In the last quarter of the last century, country lanes started to resound to the heavy thump of steam traction engines, usually preceded by a man carrying a red flag, on their way to farms where their power could be used to draw ploughs across fields, thresh wheat or undertake a number of other tasks which formerly had required the hard labour of many men and many horses. Before long, steam was replaced by the internal combustion engine, which not only made work easier on the land but also brought to the countryside, townspeople for whom the rural scene offered an escape from a busy city life.

Gradually, horse-power replaced the horse, and the great shire horses and the horses that drew the carriages, gigs and governess carts, began to disappear. So also did the landed gentry who found that their main sources of wealth now lay in mines and factories, in export and import, and whose estates were being slowly strangled by the punishing death duties introduced in 1894. These, like many other measures affecting the countryside, were decided by urban dwellers rather than countrymen and by a government minister resident in London. The turn of the century was a bad time for the countryside: wheat prices had been forced down by foreign imports, cheap mutton and lamb were arriving frozen from New Zealand and Australia, and the country people who had previously nurtured their land were leaving it for the towns and cities. Whole villages became depopulated and their buildings, some of which had stood for four hundred years and more, were left to decay.

Then, as often happens, the ill wind brought some fair weather. Townspeople, penned among their buildings and suffocating in the heavy smoke-laden air, found themselves yearning for the country life that they had lost. Industrialists from the

Mevagissey, Cornwall, 1890 (left). *The narrow street behind the inner port of this Cornish fishing village has changed little since 1890, though nowadays in summer it is crowded with tourists and the air smells not of fresh-caught fish but of chips and hamburgers. Judging from the postcards hanging at the Post Office door, visitors were not unknown in 1890 either, though they were evidently not the only source of income as the shop/Post Office also earned its keep by acting as agent for Mortimer's Plymouth Dyeing Works.*

In its heyday Mevagissey's two harbours were crowded with fishing smacks engaged in lucrative pilchard fishing. Much of the catch was sold to the Royal Navy who christened the fish 'Mevagissey Duck'. Today, the pilchards have gone and the fishing boats have turned to shark fishing and trips for holidaymakers.

Selby, North Yorkshire, 1918 (above). *The old toll bridge over the river Ouse at Selby was typical of those bridges built by private enterprise in the earliest days of road transport. The Ouse, which was navigable, helped give Selby its importance as a market town in the Middle Ages, when its chief business was wool, a trade first carried on by the Benedictine monks at the Abbey at Selby, founded in the 12th century, and later by local merchants.*

By Victorian times Selby had lost its importance as a wool town but was much visited for the fine abbey church, which was saved from destruction during the Dissolution of the monastries by being turned into the parish church.

The abbey has changed in appearance since this photograph was taken. In 1935 its two western towers were raised a whole storey, giving the building three imposing towers instead of only the central one.

Dunster, Somerset, 1909 (right and below). *The High Street at Dunster with its 17th-century Yarn Market, ivy-covered Luttrell Arms Hotel and castle has not changed much in the eighty years.*

Dunster was once a port and the tower on Conygar Hill above the village was the landmark that sailors looked for as they sailed up the river, now silted up, which connected Dunster to the sea.

Dunster Castle dates its origin from Norman times and has belonged to the Luttrell family since the 14th century. It was captured by Cromwell's troops who were billeted in the village and kept their horses in the Priory Church, once part of a monastery of Benedictine monks.

Today the High Street is full of small shops and cafes which cater for the visitors who come to visit the Castle and the fine parish church, which boasts the widest choir screen in England.

Flatford Mill, Suffolk, 1906 (above). *Willy Lotts Cottage, near Flatford Mill, inspired some of John Constable's most famous paintings, perhaps most notably* The Haywain, *and became a symbol of the English rural life that seemed to be slipping away in the torrent of the Industrial Revolution.*

Those who feared for the disappearance of the English countryside need not have worried as far as the region round Flatford Mill is concerned for today it still has the peaceful atmosphere of Constable's time. The river still flows quietly past the now refurbished cottage and through Flatford Mill, now a field study centre. What might surprise Constable were he alive today are the thousands of visitors whom his paintings attract each year to the area in which he did much of his finest work. Constable was born in East Bergholt in 1776 and painted many of the villages and mills of the countryside he grew up in, among them Dedham and Stratford St. Mary. The prosperity of the region in Constable's time was due to the wool trade which had developed in the middle ages. Today much of the local revenue comes from the tourists.

prosperous new cities began to buy up country houses and the new, affluent middle classes looked for cottages which they could refurbish as week-end homes. Moreover, these city dwellers inspired by the Romantic movement whose influence continued throughout the 19th century and well into the 20th, saw in Britain's coastline and mountains a landscape that symbolized the broader spiritual qualities of life that had been stifled by the demands of industry and commerce.

The wild areas of Britain such as the Lake District, the Pennines and the Scottish Highlands, which had first attracted the ruling classes at the beginning of the century, became the goal of all who could afford a train fare. Thousands of miles of new roads have brought the farthest corners of Britain within easy reach of the millions of us who now own cars.

Return to roots

This invasion of the countryside has brought a new prosperity to many country villages. No longer are there simple country folk ekeing out a living and feeding their children on bread and dripping in tumbledown cottages; they now have an equal share in the national wealth with their urban counterparts. There are electricity, gas and sewage, there are paved roads and, close at hand for most people, shops and supermarkets.

The complete mechanization of farming which took place after World War II was the final blow to a way of life that had continued since the Tudors At first, the machinery used was an aid to existing. farming methods but later the machines became the masters. The combine harvester, which did the work of scores of men and women, required large areas to operate in. People began to disappear from the rural landscape and the age-old skills which gave people pride in their work and a sense of community to some extent also vanished. ☐

Cattle market at Ashford, Kent, 1905. *Ashford's livestock market has served Romney Marsh and the Weald of Kent for hundreds of years and Ashford remained very much a market town until the development of the railways in the 19th century. Large, locomotive-building workshops were established, bringing an industrial element into the town, a fact emphasized in this turn-of-the-century photograph, which shows sheep and cattle standing alongside the building of an engineering company and gas lighting installed on a roadway, as yet unpaved, where the coach has not yet been ousted by the motor car.*

Today, although the railway workshops have gone, Ashford preserves some of their products in the South Eastern Steam Centre, and the industrial area of the town is still growing. The livestock market also flourishes, with markets held four days a week; the Romney Ram Show is a major event in October and the Ashford Cattle Show another one in December.

Banbury market, Oxfordshire, 1921. *Life went on in the market town of Banbury in the 1920s, when this photograph was taken, much as it had done before World War I. The motor car had not yet made any big impression on the town traffic, though some farmers were beginning to use cars and vans to transport their produce to market. The bicycle was much in evidence, however, and was rapidly replacing the horse as a means of individual transport .*

Though a bustling place today and a centre for small industries, Banbury retains the character of a pleasant country town and has preserved many of its handsome, 17th-century houses built in honey-coloured Cotswold stone. In the 19th century Banbury acquired two of the features which characterize it today: the church which replaced one blown up in the 18th century to save the townspeople the cost of repairing it, and the Market Cross which took the place of the one destroyed by Puritans in the 17th century.

Market day in Skipton, North Yorkshire, 1890s (left). *The splendid width of Skipton's High Street, given over in this photograph to the activity of market day, is a sure sign that Skipton has been a market town for a long time – centuries, in fact. In the Middle Ages, when wool was England's main export, sheep reared on the surrounding hills were brought to Skipton market for sale. The market probably grew up round the great Norman castle, built in the 11th century and for more than six hundred years the* home of the Clifford family, Earls of Cumberland. Clifford family tombs may still be seen in the parish church of St Mary, whose square tower rises above the end of the High Street.

Skipton is still a busy market town (above), *and the stalls of its general market are set up along the High Street several days a week; the livestock market has been moved elsewhere. The Women's Institute keeps alive the tradition of the farmer's wife coming to market with its own weekly market, held in the old Covered Market off the High Street.*

Great Yarmouth, Norfolk, 1908. *When this picture was taken Great Yarmouth was not very different from the market town that Charles Dickens stayed in, at the Royal Hotel, in 1848. Electricity had arrived, as we can see, to power the trams and light the streets, but the fabric of the town was unchanged. The market was situated in the busiest part of the town to the south of the church of St Nicholas, though by 1908 the town on the Yare river had extended seawards over the city walls and was becoming more famous as a seaside resort than a market town. The port on the river Yare continued to be active, however, with both commercial and pleasure craft.*

In World War II a great part of the old town was destroyed by German bombers attacking the important river port, and the narrow alleys of the old quarter called The Rows almost disappeared under the devastating weight of the bombardment, although some were later rebuilt. In fact, Dickens would not recognize modern Great Yarmouth at all, for the whole of the sea front, virtually empty in his day, is now a vast holiday playground with giant fun fairs, roller-skating rinks, boating lakes, pier entertainments and every other kind of holiday fun, for the thousands of summer visitors who arrive to enjoy the fine sandy beaches.

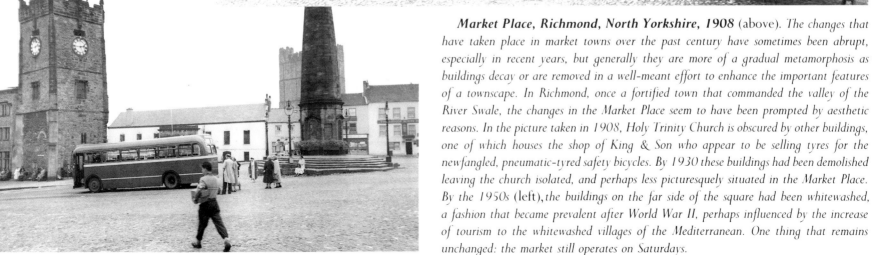

Market Place, Richmond, North Yorkshire, 1908 (above). *The changes that have taken place in market towns over the past century have sometimes been abrupt, especially in recent years, but generally they are more of a gradual metamorphosis as buildings decay or are removed in a well-meant effort to enhance the important features of a townscape. In Richmond, once a fortified town that commanded the valley of the River Swale, the changes in the Market Place seem to have been prompted by aesthetic reasons. In the picture taken in 1908, Holy Trinity Church is obscured by other buildings, one of which houses the shop of King & Son who appear to be selling tyres for the newfangled, pneumatic-tyred safety bicycles. By 1930 these buildings had been demolished leaving the church isolated, and perhaps less picturesquely situated in the Market Place. By the 1950s* (left), *the buildings on the far side of the square had been whitewashed, a fashion that became prevalent after World War II, perhaps influenced by the increase of tourism to the whitewashed villages of the Mediterranean. One thing that remains unchanged: the market still operates on Saturdays.*

Loch Lubnaig, Scotland 1890s (left). *The bent loch, as Loch Lubnaig is called, lies to the north of Callander and near the region known as the Trossachs. This became an extremely popular destination for Victorians who found their perfect image of Scotland along the pine-clad shores. Lubnaig being near Callander received its share of visitors but mostly those who preferred to get away from crowds like the two lone oarsmen in the photograph. The lake lies at the bottom of the Leny pass and the stony hills that surround it have the austere beauty of Scottish Highland scenery but with the picturesque counterpoint of trees growing along grassy banks at the water's edge.*

Ross-on-Wye, Hereford and Worcester, 1901 (right). *Ross-on-Wye is a typical English riverside town set in a wide valley in which the river Wye meanders between grassy tree-fringed banks. It has long been popular as a centre for exploring the nearby Welsh border and Black Mountains and for excursions on the river such as that being enjoyed by the couple in the photograph. Ross is more than a visitors' town however, and has a lively cattle market as well as a general market in an attractive and ancient building in the town centre. In 1901, coracles were still in use, as can be seen, and perhaps were used to ferry visitors across the river.*

Bala, Gwynedd, 1931. *The landscape around the village of Bala in North Wales is as varied as in any part of Britain. In the distance rise the barren mountains suitable only for raising sheep or goats. Here the private areas of land are marked by stone walls or, nowadays, by wire fences. In the valleys the land is fertile and used for agriculture like the one in the foreground where sheaves of grain are piled together to await the thresher. The agricultural fields are marked by hedgerows traditionally of hazel, beech and holly. Between them are patches of the ancient forests that covered Britain, today*

these remnants serve as windbreaks and nature reserves. Around the village are market gardens providing fresh vegetables for the inhabitants of the village who may if lucky catch a Lake Bala trout for their dinner.

Today Bala has changed little from the balmy days before the War shown here. The tourist industry has made use of the lake and housing has encroached upon the fields surrounding the town, but there is still peace and tranquillity to be found in the rolling hills and placid lakes that have always been a feature of the area.

Skipton Woods, North Yorkshire, 1911 (left). Skipton lies amid the beautiful scenery of the Aire Valley which cuts through the Pennines at the southern end of North Yorkshire. The town is built around the castle remodelled by the redoubtable Lady Anne Clifford in the 17th century and which withstood a three-year siege by Cromwell's troops. Once a centre of the wool trade, Skipton became a place much visited for the natural beauty of its surroundings. Near the town are the Skipton Woods, a leafy glade with rushing torrents popular among those who, like the couple on the bridge, are not looking for anything more demanding than a quiet and perhaps romantic stroll. More energetic spirits nowadays come to Skipton as a base for vigorous walks over the Pennines to the precipitous limestone amphitheatre of Malham Cove or to the waterfalls of Gordale Scar.

Ambleside, Cumbria, 1886 (right). The sure-footed lady in her long skirt and bustle evidently feels no fear as she crosses the stepping stones over a stream to Ambleside at the northern end of Lake Windermere. Her parasol might also be helping her balance but the real reason she is holding it aloft is that she does not want to be tanned by the rays of the sun. In Victorian days it was not fashionable to have a brown skin, perhaps because this was associated with the working classes who spent much of their time out of doors, and therefore a white skin was regarded as a mark of gentility.

This scene, photographed by Francis Frith, emphasizes the extensive use made of the slate readily available in the northern parts of the Lake District; the house is solidly constructed of local stone and its roof is made of slates which were split and cut in local quarries. In 1886, Ambleside was a quiet village from which visitors walked to Rydal Water and Grasmere to visit Wordsworth's two homes. Today it is a busy tourist centre thronged with the motor cars and tourist buses of many thousands of visitors.

Llanberis, Gwynedd, North Wales, 1896
(above and right). *The railway that takes summer visitors to the summit of Mount Snowdon has its terminus at Llanberis. The village, spread out along low-lying land between Llyn Padarn and Llyn Peris, is surrounded by steep, rugged slopes. Today, however, some of these, on the north side of Llyn Padarn from which this picture was taken, are scarred by quarries first worked in 1809.*

From Llanberis a road rises through the narrow pass to Pen-y-Pass Youth hostel. This is the start of two of the walking tracks to the summit which became popular during the 19th century when mountain walking became an activity which grew in popularity among the many residents of industrial cities who sought in the countryside an escape from the urban environment.

Cheddar Gorge, 1888. *Since the picture, shown on the left, of the Cheddar Gorge was taken, trees and undergrowth have softened the austere grandeur of the limestone canyon, (below) though the National Trust is now making a big effort to clear the vegetation and restore some of the Gorge's original splendour.*

To the Victorians, this dramatic cleft in the Mendip Hills fulfilled all their yearnings for the kind of nature extolled by the Romantic poets and which many travelled to Switzerland to enjoy. The cliffs, the rock pinnacles, the waterfalls, the caves all seemed to symbolize the wild nature which the Almighty had created for man to enjoy and to tame.

Modern visitors to the Gorge have a more pragmatic approach and use the cliffs for practice climbs, and visit the caves for entertainment. The amplifiers, floodlights and holograms, and the abundance of souvenir shops and cafés do not, however, entirely eradicate the feeling of awe that the natural phenomenon of the Cheddar Gorge arouses.

Honister Crag, Cumbria, 1893. *The Honister Pass, which runs from Derwent Water to Buttermere via Borrowdale, is a wild and inhospitable place even today when there is a motor road to make the journey easy. In 1893, the crossing of the pass by horse-drawn vehicles was a major undertaking and took one full day in good weather. Few people would have wanted to attempt it for pleasure but some had work to be done in the slate quarries to which the zig-zag paths seen in the photograph lead. Today, the quarries no longer operate but the paths are still used by walkers. The track seen at the bottom of the valley is now a paved road often crowded with cars doing the circular tour from Ambleside to Buttermere which is reached from the summit of the Honister Pass by a narrow 3 in 4 road with spectacular views of Crummock Water and Buttermere.*

Wynds Point, Great Malvern, Hereford and Worcester, 1893 (right). *The Inn at Wynds Point was a favourite stopping place for walkers and the more sedentary folk who enjoyed carriage drives over the Malvern Hills. One of the attractions nearby was the Worcestershire Beacon, a hilltop from which 15 counties are visible as well as the towers of several abbeys.*

The Malvern Hills became popular in Victorian times for medicinal springs which are still providing their pure waters, in bottled form, to the discerning throughout Britain. Among the famous people attracted over the years to the wooded hills that overlook the Severn Valley to the east have been Daniel Defoe, Oliver Goldsmith and Jenny Lind, who is buried in the Great Malvern cemetery. Edward Elgar also lived in the Malvern Hills and some of his music captures the quiet, pastoral atmosphere of this idyllic English landscape. He is buried at Little Malvern.

Ilkley Moor, West Yorkshire, 1914 (right). *Ilkley Moor's reputation for bleakness is summed up in the local song about a man who went out on the moor with a hat and died, becoming food for worms who in turn were eaten by ducks which finally provided a tasty supper for the dead man's companions. Stretching high above the Wharfe Valley, the area of the moors was of strategic importance when the Romans built the town of Olicana at the highest point above the river where the town of Ilkley stands today. In Victorian times, the area had a short-lived popularity as a spa because of the mineral springs found in the limestone hills, and visitors enjoyed the walks across the moors then as they do today, no doubt visiting such familiar landmarks as the Cow and Calf Rocks, the White Wells and the circle of rocks known as the Twelve Apostles, as well as the nearby ruins of Bolton Abbey.*

Towns of Industry

At the beginning of the 19th century most of the towns and cities of Britain today were hardly more than large villages or market towns. The decay of agriculture and the growth of industry brought the population into towns which grew in an uncontrolled and idiosyncratic manner, but with imposing city centres in which was reflected the architecture of the gothic period and the Italian Renaissance.

Lime Street, Liverpool, 1890. *In 1890 Liverpool was at the peak of its power, transatlantic steamships and cargo boats bound for all parts of the world lined its quaysides and the new Lime Street station, opened in 1870, towered over the massive classical St George's Hall, completed in 1854. It seemed then that Britain's dominant world role, which developed after the defeat of Napoleon by Wellington, who stands on the column in the far distance of this photograph, would go on forever. A new form of transport was, however, to erode Liverpool's supremacy as a port. When airlines began to operate in Europe between the Wars, the challenge was negligible but, after World War II, the popularity of sea transport faded rapidly and Liverpool's docks were emptied. The spirit of Liverpool remained intact, however, and now the city is struggling to restore some of its former affluence through other activities, such as tourism.*

Town Hall, Leeds, 1894 (left). *The magnificent Leeds Town Hall was built in 1858 by Cuthbert Broderick and reflects the classical line followed by some architects of the period. When this picture was taken, the soot and grime common to cities of the Industrial North had blackened the stonework, but this has now been restored to its original colour. Like most town halls of the affluent, northern industrial cities, the one at Leeds expresses both a supreme self-confidence and a preoccupation with the finer things of life, as portrayed in the frieze round the building which depicts art, poetry and music, as well as industry and science. The virtually obligatory stone lions, which guarded almost every public monument, were a symbol of Britain's imperial power and its role as a guardian of the Pax Britannica.*

Crown Street, Halifax, 1896 (below). *Situated on the southern flanks of the Pennines near the coalfields that powered its mills, Halifax was destined to be a leading cloth town of the 19th century, having been a wool-trading town for centuries. The mills sprang up rapidly in the valley of the Hebble and the vast cloth market, the Piece Hall, dominated the centre of the town. Today, some of the Piece Hall's 300 rooms are a museum displaying textile machinery. Crown Street was a busy street in the centre of the town, as it still is.*

Today, Halifax is regarded as one of the most imaginatively redeveloped towns in Britain, with a market that has been modernized while preserving many original features. Its most striking office development is the ultra-modern building of the Halifax Building Society.

The growth of industrial towns in the past 150 years has had a profound effect on the life-style and character of the British people. The majority have become urban dwellers, growing up in noisy crowded streets polluted by dust and smoke, instead of among the sounds and smells of nature and the rhythms of its seasons. For this reason alone, the formative period of many children's lives in 1830 was very different from that in 1880. The earlier child was perhaps more ignorant, except in the ways of natural life more aware of his immediate neighbours and less of the world at large, more resigned to his destiny and blissfully unconscious of the fact that life could be regarded as a ladder up which he could climb to material and social success. The 1880 child was more likely to be able to read and write, to measure his life against a national mark and to have developed desires for the comfort and well-being of himself, his family and even of his class, which would never have occurred to his father.

Not everyone, of course, experienced such changes of life-style. It took time for measures aimed at improving living conditions to come to fruition, and indeed such changes are still taking place, but overall the difference in life expectations experienced by most people between the start of Victoria's reign and the end was significant.

The new character of the people was moulded by their lives in the towns and cities which had grown rapidly since the beginning of the Industrial Revolution. The transformation was swift: at the beginning of the 19th century, 11 million people lived in Britain, by the end there were more than 20 million; today there are nearly 55 million. Thus, a relatively small agricultural country in a very short time was transformed into a teeming urban one, with country life which had evolved over centuries becoming totally subservient to the city economy and way of life.

Birmingham

Modern Birmingham bears little resemblance to the industrial city of the 19th century in which a greater variety of manufacturing workshops had thrived than in any other city in Britain. Today, the grime and squalor of the Victorian industrial city have disappeared and the centre of the city has been replanned. One focal point is the Bull-Ring, near the point where New Street and High Street meet. The Bull-Ring is a vast three-acre area of shops, restaurants and other city amenities. A link with the past remains, however, in the market which was founded in the 12th century and continues to serve the modern city. Near the Bull-Ring is the cylindrical Rotunda building, which will be demolished in yet another redevelopment of the city centre in the near future.

Corporation Street, 1890 (below) . *Corporation Street, with its fine Victorian facades, is still an important Birmingham thoroughfare, though slightly overwhelmed today by the massive redevelopment of the New Street and Bull-ring shopping centre. Corporation Street was built between 1878 and 1882 in a former slum area and became a fashionable street full of fine buildings, many of which have now been demolished. At its northern end, however, there are still many examples of notable Victorian architecture, including the Law Courts by Sir Aston Webb and Ingress Bell, built between 1887 and 1891 and the Methodist Central Hall (1903) by E.J. Harper.*

The Town Hall, Paradise Street, 1896 (below and right). *The Victorian view along Paradise Street no longer exists for the church, Christchurch, was demolished at the turn of the century. The Roman, temple-style Town Hall is still there, however, as a reminder that Victorian Englishmen saw themselves as latter-day Romans carrying the same onerous responsibility of Roman senators as rulers of the earth and protectors of civilisation.*

Today, the Roman Temple is the home of the Birmingham Symphony Orchestra, which maintains the fine musical traditions of the city. The first world performance of Mendelssohn's Elijah took place here in 1846.

The Birmingham Art Gallery, 1896 (above). *The Birmingham Art Gallery forms part of a large block dominated by the Council House built between 1874 and 1879, and embodying the concepts of local government set out by Joseph Chamberlain during the years he was Mayor of Birmingham. The whole complex of buildings in the centre of Birmingham makes a stimulating contrast to the modern Bull-Ring development. The splendid 19th-century edifices range over a wide variety of styles, including the Roman-temple-style Town Hall built by Joseph Hansom, after whom the cabs were named, a French-chateau-style post office, and the Renaissance-style Council House and Art Gallery.*

Housing conditions

At first, the growing towns and cities evolved without any planning or direction for the Victorian ethos rejoiced in free enterprise, free trade and freedom from government interference in peoples' lives. There was no control over urban development or the quality of new housing. There were no sewage, garbage disposal or health regulations. The slums that provided Charles Dickens with many of his settings and Gustave Doré with many subjects for his drawings were all too often the rather distressing result.

Though local government did little about the squalor on its doorstep, many officials in fact believing that Britain's industrial success would put such matters right by its own impetus, a few private citizens did take action to improve living conditions for at least some of the people. Among them were Octavia Hill who, with John Ruskin's encouragement, devoted her life to the provision of better housing for the poor, as well as helping to found the National Trust; George Peabody, an American businessman living in Britain, many of whose estates for the working poor are still in use in London; W.H. Lever, later Lord Leverhulme, creator of Port Sunlight; Sir Titus Salt; and the Cadbury family who built workers' estates near their factories.

Growth of local government

Despite these individual efforts, it was obvious that local government would eventually have to shoulder responsibility for the sprawling new towns. The situation was summed up by Joseph Chamberlain, during his term as Mayor of Birmingham in 1873-76, when he claimed that the role of local councils was to serve the interests of the people. At the time, this was a radical view but it became the central core of local government

Queen Square, Wolverhampton, 1910 (above). *The area around Queen Square became the entertainment centre of Wolverhampton in Victorian and Edwardian times, with the Empire Palace (later the Hippodrome) being a focal point. Like most of Wolverhampton, the square had a solid Victorian air about it which gave it character. Since then many changes have taken place in Wolverhampton. Some of the Victorian landmarks still remain, including the Royal London Buildings in Princes Street and the fine neo-classical art gallery and museum in Lichfield Street. Latterly, in tune with a new mood of appreciation for past architecture, efforts have been made to conserve areas of historic interest such as around St John Square and nearby Cheapside.*

Butcher's Row, Coventry, 1892 (right). *This picturesque little street, was demolished in 1936 to make way for the road widening scheme which swept away both Little and Great Butcher's Row and replaced them with Trinity Street and the department store 'Owen and Owen'.*

The city of Coventry has a long and chequered past. Coventry was founded back in the 7th century – only the fourth city to be established in England – under the patronage and protection of a Saxon convent, which was destroyed around 1016.

Towards the turn of the century the car industry started to grow to eventually become the centre of the motor industry. It was in Coventry that many of the famous names like Lanchester and Alvis started their factories.

philosophy, eventually involving every aspect of services to the local community.

If local government were to play a greater part in providing local services, it would need administrative buildings. The period from the 1870s consequently saw such an extensive programme of municipal building as to change the face of the centres of many towns and cities. There had been institutional buildings before then, of course: halls and exchanges for conducting businesses and trades that had been based on the traditional Market Halls and Guildhalls, and often built in a style dating back to the Middle Ages. But something different was required for the new age of industry and commerce.

Municipal architecture

In their travels round Europe, the new leaders of Britain had been impressed by the European heirs of the successful city states of the late Middle Ages and the Renaissance where much magnificent architecture and opulent works of art still survived. They felt a greater sense of kinship with the commercial and cultural cities of Florence, Sienna, Venice, Bruges and Ghent, than with the works of Nash, Adam and their ilk who served the landed gentry, and they were anxious to establish new symbols for their industrial age. So they opted for the eclectic styles which are characteristic of 19th-century British cities.

The Town Halls built from the 1870s onward vied with each other in grandeur and ostentation, standing out among humbler dwellings like cathedrals and creating much the effect that the Roman forum must have had on the Romans. In fact, it does not take much imagination on a stroll round the old civic centre of Birmingham with its Roman temples, Renaissance palazzo, and French chateau, to feel oneself in some magnificent film set for an epic on the history of Western civilisation.

Coventry Cathedral, c.1900 (left) *and today* (right, below). *Whilst the old cathedral of St Michael, bombed out in 1940, has become a symbol of Coventry's quiet and learned past, its new one has come to represent all that is modern about the city. Those who founded the first cathedral and abbey churches in Britain usually called upon the finest craftsmen available to enrich their buildings, and such places as Canterbury Cathedral or York Minster became show-cases of the best that man could offer God in the way of art and architecture.*

Coventry's new cathedral, designed by Sir Basil Spence and built between 1954 and 1962, continues the tradition. Pictured here is the famous statue of St Michael hovering against the east wall by the sculptor Sir Jacob Epstein (whose figure of Christ, Ecce Homo, sits in judgement over the ruins of the old cathedral next door). The huge stained glass window is the work of John Piper and the largest tapestry in the world, hanging from the ceiling to the floor behind the altar, is by Graham Sutherland. Benjamin Britten wrote his War Requiem *for the new cathedral's dedication in 1962. Coventry's modern cathedral proves the church is still a major patron of the arts – as it has been since Christianity in Britain began.*

Cornmarket, Derby, 1896 (left and below). *The Cornmarket is a reminder that Derby was once a small market town. The arrival of the Midland Railway in 1839 altered its destiny and it rapidly became an industrial centre. In 1876, the Great Northern Railway also extended its line to Derby, thus making the town a railway centre as well as a manufacturer of fine china.*

The railway heritage is continued at the British Railway Research Centre and its experimental laboratories which, with the Crown Derby and Rolls Royce factories, ensure Derby's continuing prosperity. Today, see below, Cornmarket is a busy shopping centre, which includes Sadlers Gate and St James.

Beyond Cornmarket is Irongate which leads to the cathedral, formerly the parish church of All Saints whose pinnacled tower was built in 1525.

Dale Street, Liverpool, 1887 (left). *Dale Street, which leads from the centre of Liverpool to Water Street and the Mersey quaysides, has always been a busy thoroughfare. In 1887 its cobbled surface echoed to the rumble of carts and trains travelling to and from the docks where ocean-going steamships unloaded their cargoes. Liverpool's Town Hall, with its clock and spire, is still a landmark in Dale Street. Built in 1754 by John Wood, architect of much of the city of Bath, it contains many treasures, including 28-foot chandeliers in the ballroom. Hard hit by terrible bombing in War War II and the subsequent decline in ocean-going shipping, Liverpool has developed a number of tourist attractions such as the International Garden Festival, a fine maritime museum and recently the new extension of the Tate Gallery.*

Town Hall, Sheffield, 1902 (below). *Until recently, Sheffield's Town Hall possessed the tallest tower in the city but it has been surpassed by the 255-foot Arts Tower of Sheffield University's Western bank site. This is symbolic of the city which has always looked ahead since Elizabeth I's reign when it became famous for the quality of the weapons and agricultural implements it produced.*

World fame came to the city when the Industrial Revolution introduced better and faster methods of manufacturing steel. The demands for Sheffield steel increased employment in the city, which equally soon suffered the fate of most industrial conurbations of the 19th century with misery and squalor becoming rampant. By the late 19th century the city began to recover and in recent years has been considerably rebuilt in contemporary style.

Next to the town halls were erected buildings dedicated to culture, their significance either being spelled out in large letters across their porticos – 'Art', 'Poetry', 'Music', and so on – or expressed by impressive statues of female bodies personifying the Muses. These galleries, museums, libraries and concert halls, as well as being the embodiment of the aspirations of local councils to raise cultural standards, became depositories of gifts from benefactors who had accumulated collections of porcelain, silver, antiques, statuary and paintings, often gathered on their travels abroad.

Then, too, buildings had to be constructed for the police, a force which had been established by Sir Robert Peel back in 1829, fire brigades, and state schools. The building activity also extended to churches, both among the supporters of the established Church and the Dissenters, who disapproved of the Anglican establishment; there was much new building and refurbishing of old churches, sometimes to the detriment of their ancient fabric.

Growing populations in the towns and cities also created other opportunities. Shops, which had hitherto been small general stores, now diversified to serve the varied demands of the public; the butcher, the baker and the candlestick maker all flourished in the new towns and larger stores began to appear in the principal streets, forerunners of great department stores.

Late Victorian architects

The fever of construction which seized late Victorian society benefited architects, many of whom won a place in the history of Britain for their striking work.

They included Cuthbert Broderick, creator of Leeds Town Hall and Corn Exchange, and of Scarborough's huge Italianate Grand Hotel; Sir Aston Webb who, with Ingress Bell, designed the Law

Manchester

In the early part of the 19th century Manchester had about 150,000 inhabitants may of whom worked in the cotton mills. By 1853 Manchester was reorganised as a city and by 1894 the opening of the Manchester Ship Canal had made it the most important inland port in the world and the third largest of all British ports. There is little of old Manchester left today, the city having been redeveloped progressively since the mid-19th century, but particularly after the First World War when much of the centre was swept away. There is the fine church of St Ann and the Georgian terraces of St. John Street, but unfortunately little else remains. The decline of the cotton business and of shipping had a dire effect on Britain's great centre of manufacturing, but many new high technology industries are rapidly replacing the old and restoring Manchester's economic and social fortunes.

Piccadilly 1887. This was the year of Queen Victoria's Golden Jubilee, and Manchester was advertising a Royal Jubilee exhibition on the poster against the railings of the Royal Infirmary. This monolith of a building was founded in 1752 and rebuilt in Oxford Road in 1908 to make room for present-day Piccadilly.

Today, the area is almost unrecognizable. The old buildings have been replaced by modern concrete blocks, the cobbles by a smooth road surface and the horse-drawn buses and hansom cabs by double-deckers and motor cars. In other parts of the city many of the monumental buildings of the 19th century remain, however, notably the vast Gothic Town Hall, designed by Alfred Waterhouse and completed in 1877, and the City Art Gallery, which was originally known, in true Victorian style, as the Royal Manchester Institution for the Promotion of Literature, Science and the Arts.

The Royal Infirmary, 1886 (above). *The huge Manchester Royal Infirmary, which was demolished in 1908 to make way for the Piccadilly Gardens, was a splendid example of Victorian civic architecture. Based on the classical style, which Victorians made their own after visits to Italy, it has the ponderous self-consciousness of Victorian society, yet it also represented their concern with good works.*

In this photograph, hansom cabs queue to pick up visitors emerging from the Infirmary and an itinerant food-seller stands with his handcart near the people seated in the square.

Piccadilly Gardens 1950s. *The Gardens are little changed today from this 1950s photograph. The shops have more modern frontages and the hair-styles have changed, but this leafy oasis in the busy city centre is still a popular meeting place.*

Royal Exchange, Manchester, 1886. *The Manchester Royal Exchange building today houses a theatre and restaurant but in the 19th century it was the heart of the world's cotton manufacturing industry. The combination of a moist climate, rapidly available coal, and the invention of steam power and cotton-spinning machinery, gave Manchester a world monopoly on cotton manufacture. The supremacy in cotton, which made the city one of the most affluent in Britain, declined as a result of the failure of supplies of raw material during the American Civil War and later also because of competition from other countries.*

Courts in Birmingham, the new east facade of Buckingham Palace, and the Queen Victoria memorial in front of it; H. R. Yeovil Thomason, designer of the Council House also in Birmingham; Alfred Waterhouse, architect of the Manchester Town Hall; George Gilbert Scott, one of the leading practitioners of the Neo-Gothic style, who designed St Pancras station, and many other famous buildings.

Pubs and music halls

As people found that improving conditions gave them more time and money, so they began to demand somewhere to spend them – or, at least, men did, for women still rarely went out. Public houses flourished, each with its own clientele who regarded it much as the wealthier members of the middle classes regarded their club. The public house was a place of recreation and for conducting business in a friendly manner over a drink or two.

For more boisterous amusements, men went to the music halls to enjoy hearing risqué songs and comedians lampooning authority. In the big cities, the music halls attracted large audiences. At the Alhambra or Empire in London, for instance, aristocrats rubbed shoulders with commoners, and probably unwittingly shared some of the 60,000 prostitutes who frequented the area.

Patterns of town life

The patterns of town life established in the 19th century have been perpetuated. Local government has spread its net ever wider, gathering in every kind of public service and social activity. With the decay of the industries that created the cities and gave them half a century of affluence, the responsibilities of local government have increased.

Those vast acres of 19th-century housing are now badly decayed, requiring the demolition and reconstruction of large areas. Drainage and sewage,

Church Street, Accrington, Lancashire, 1899 (below). *At the turn of the century, Accrington was doing well from the manufacture of the red bricks that were in demand for the millions of homes being built in the suburbia of British towns, as well as from its cotton and fabrics business. It was also doing well in the clothing business, which was a competitive one. As we can see, the Cash Clothing store in this photograph needed to display its goods on the pavement to attract customers.*

Today, Accrington continues to be an industrial town but it is also well known for the Haworth Art Gallery, containing the finest collection of Tiffany glass in Britain.

The Art Gallery, Preston, Lancashire, 1903 (right). *The dramatic quality of two of Preston's Victorian buildings are appropriate for a city that has had an eventful history. Charles I's forces were defeated here by Cromwell and nearly a century later the town was taken by Bonnie Prince Charlie. Preston's greatest glory was, however, given by two other men: John Horrocks, who set up the first cotton mill in 1786, and Richard Arkwright, whose spinning jenny revolutionized the textile industry.*

Today, Preston looks to other kinds of industry and, because of its convenient situation near motorways, has become a centre for the service and distributive trades.

Newcastle-upon-Tyne from Rabbit Banks, 1898. *After 1921 the multiplicity of railways that had been launched by entrepreneurs at the time of the railway boom of the 1880s had been much reduced and an Act of Parliament rationalised the remaining companies into four regions, the Great Western, Southern, London Midland Scottish, and London North Eastern. The latter ran to Newcastle whose railway terminus is served by Robert Stephenson's high-level bridge shown in this picture. The bridge was built in 1849 and carries the railway and a road 34 metres above the river, and was the largest bridge in the world when completed. There are now five bridges over the Tyne all within a kilometre of each other, two of which – the King Edward Railway Bridge built in*

1906 and the Tyne (road) Bridge built in 1926 – had yet to be built and would not have been visible from Rabbit Banks when this photograph was taken. Through the busy station passed incoming and outgoing passenger traffic and the goods from inland industrial cities destined for the ships at the Newcastle quaysides.

The railway station is still busy with fast trains that connect Newcastle to other major cities of Britain. Newcastle also has an international airport and its port still provides transport for both passengers and freight to the N. Europe with which it has been trading since the time of the Vikings. Thus, Newcastle is the centre of the largest manufacturing area of the north east and the gateway for trade between Britain and Scandinavia.

inadequate for today's population, need to be improved, new uses must be found for land once occupied by factories that have closed down, while others have to be built to suit new types of business. In addition, the care of the increasingly aged population, which will become more acute as we move into the latter part of the 20th century, has caused a need for much more sophisticated social services.

As the responsibilities of local government have widened so, ironically, have their resources diminished. Towns and cities, whose former affluence and pride is reflected in their 19th-century public buildings, are finding themselves with increasing problems, especially in the inner cities, increasingly deserted as most of those who work in them choose to live in the suburbs and countryside on their outskirts.

It remains to be seen whether the present campaign to regenerate the inner cities will reverse a trend, or even whether it is necessarily one that should be reversed; perhaps it is just another sign of the relentless tide of change which has always carried us before it and which flows on to other high water marks beyond our vision. □

Dean Street, Newcastle-upon-Tyne, 1898 (above). *The railway viaduct which crosses Dean Street was built in the 19th century to carry trains from the Central Station eastwards. This was the second bridge built across the thoroughfare that ran from the quaysides to Market Street, the Side then St Nicholas Street, spanned by an earlier bridge which cut through the castle built by Henry II. Under the arch of the viaduct St Nicholas's cathedral can be seen but its 15th-century spire is obscured by the span of the bridge. The houses in the street represented many periods of Newcastle's long history from the Tudor building in which Mr S. Broadbent carried on his oyster business to the Victorian edifice on the left where Mr W. Brennan sold cigars.*

Today, (**right**) *the viaduct is still there but many of the buildings on the right hand side have been replaced. The agreeably proportioned building on the left with its paired rounded arch windows has been fortunately preserved.*

Shambles, York, 1909 (below). *The picturesque Shambles provides the modern visitor with a glimpse of a street in medieval times except that today the clean, attractive shops are full of souvenirs and crafts and no one is likely to empty slops out of a first-floor window! Unlike other northern cities, York was relatively untouched by the Industrial Revolution and therefore retained its ancient walls and buildings, thus providing us with one of the most complete pictures of urban life as it was when Britain was still an agricultural country.*

Today, the market square off the Shambles retains a lusty medieval atmosphere and so does Stonegate further west. Both are pedestrian precincts leading off Petergate, a narrow street divided into High and Low sections, which lead to the magnificent Minster and the great impressive stone gate of Bootham bar.

Coney Street, York, 1909. (below). *Coney Street, which runs parallel to the river Ouse, was a fashionable street in Edwardian times, as we can see by the ladies in their elegant hats on the left of the picture. York was at the centre of the industrial north but escaped the explosion of factories that happened to the rest of Yorkshire. It remained a fashionable city to settle in, for those who had already made their money, away from the workers they employed in their factories.*

As can be seen in this picture, in York for the well off, this was the age of the bicycle and of the motor car, though carriages had not yet been forced off the roads. The gentleman, on the right of his rakish motor car with his back-to-front cap and goggles, looks, however, like an early speedstar whose only concern is to get there faster and, of course, first!

Bridge Street, Chester, 1895 (right). *Like York, Chester retained its character as all around it the Industrial Revolution raged on Merseyside and the surrounding area. Also like York it was a favourite place for those who had made their money in industry to buy large homes away from the factories which provided them with their wealth.*

The ancient cathedral city was a Roman town and its present walls were built during medieval times on the old foundations. Of all the cities of Britain, it provides the best picture of Tudor urban development. Its half-timbered buildings represent the architecture of a time when forests were still abundant and stone scarce, except in certain areas. The cathedral and its attendant monastery and churches – of which St Peter's, shown in this photograph of Bridge Street, was one – were the focal points of Chester life until the Dissolution of the Monasteries.

The Town Hall, Northampton, 1922. *The Gothic splendour of the Northampton Town Hall is overpowering – which is what it was intended to be. Victorian municipal leaders based their ideas of local government on the successful city states of Europe in which massive buildings stood for authority and inspiration to the common people. Apart from the town hall, Northampton's 19th-century dignitaries left little of note.*

In 1968 Northampton was selected for a new town development and since then has grown considerably, with many other industries being attracted into the area to add to the traditional footwear industry in which it is still Britain's leading manufacturer of men's shoes. By 1990 it is estimated that the new business development in and around the city will support a population of 180,000.

The Market Place, Blackburn, 1894. *The people at the Blackburn market in 1894 would not recognize the modern town (inset); there is even a concrete tower that stands on the site of the Italian-style stone clock tower. Whatever the aesthetics of the matter, there is no doubt that the Victorian tower has a personality.*

Blackburn was a weaving town as long ago as the 15th century when Flemish weavers arrived to set up in business but the town's major expansion took place in the 19th century. The invention of the spinning jenny and Crompton mule (both in the Lewis Textile Museum in Blackburn) brought wealth to Blackburn cotton mills and funded the buildings of the town.

Modern factories now crowd the banks of the Leeds Canal along which barges once transported Blackburn's cotton but there are one or two old mills still operating and the canal is now used for pleasure rather then commerce.

Commercial Street, Newport, 1901 (below). *Commercial Street, though one of the principal streets of Newport, was a quiet place when this photograph was taken in 1901, with only a cart and a horse tram to disturb the jay walkers. The street leads on to Commercial Road and the Transport Bridge, which had not been built when this picture was taken. When it was in operation in 1906 it was regarded as one of the technological marvels of the period as it carried vehicles and pedestrians across the River Usk.*

After the decay of the coal mining and heavy industry, which had created it, Newport turned to other activities and the centre of the town was redesigned with a vast retail shopping centre, the largest in South Wales.

Wind Street, Swansea, 1908 (right). *Wind Street in the centre of Swansea, leads from the harbour road past the remains of the castle in Castle Street and on to the High Street. The castle was a fortified manor belonging to the Bishop of Gower in the 14th century; by the 19th century it had become part of the fabric of the street and a convenient site for the clock by which the shoppers of Swansea checked their watches.*

The gentleman on the pedestal is Henry Hussey Vivian, later Lord Swansea, a great benefactor of the city. His statue has been removed and now stands in Ferrara Place. Swansea was heavily bombed in World War II and much of the city, including Castle Street, has now been completely rebuilt.

High Street, Cardiff, 1893 and today (inset right). *St Mary Street and High Street leading to Cardiff Castle have always been very busy shopping streets with fine buildings like the Venetian-style Victorian 'Palazzo' on the right which was partly occupied by a clothier, a sign of the greater affluence of society at the end of the Victorian era. It is obvious from the reaction of the towns-people that photography was still a novelty and the sight of one of Francis Frith's men with his large bellows camera mounted on a solid, wooden tripid caused considerable interest in this Welsh city.*

Since 1893 Cardiff has suffered various setbacks; trade diminished after World War I and much of the city was destroyed by bombing in World War II but a new city has arisen from the old and many of the historic buildings have been preserved.

Cardiff has always been the powerhouse of the South Wales industry. Its docks have transported coal and goods all over the world. Today, the docks are mostly disused and falling into ruin, like many of Britain's ports, but there is a vigorous scheme for their regeneration now in progress.

Cardiff Castle, South Glamorgan 1950s. *Cardiff was a place of strategic importance from ancient times. The Romans built a fort there by the River Taff in AD 75, in the first instance to control the local people, but later to defend them against attacks from Irish pirates. After the Romans left, their castle fell into ruins and was not rebuilt until the Normans arrived. The town received its charter from Elizabeth I, but its real growth and importance came with the dawn of the industrial age and the exploitation of the South Wales coalfields.*

Argyle Street, Glasgow, 1890 (below). *Argyle Street, running east and west from the British Rail Central Station, is one of Glasgow's busiest shopping streets, as it was in 1897 when this photograph was taken. The area around the station has a number of splendid Victorian buildings including an iron frame and glass warehouse and the Egyptian Hall, to the North-east of the station the centre of Glasgow at George Square boasts the Renaissance-style city chambers, built by William Young in 1883-88, which provides the grandeur associated with Victorian municipal architecture. The decay of shipping and heavy industry in the 20th century has brought traumatic changes to what was once one of the greatest industrial cities in the world.*

Charing Cross, Glasgow, 1897 (right). *Charing Cross lies at the western edge of central Glasgow, along which runs the M8 motorway. When Francis Frith's photographer took this picture the fastest vehicles on the road were the trams and no doubt the residents of the Grand Hotel complained about them.*

The buildings in the Charing Cross area are typical of the solid Victorian style of much of Glasgow's development during the time of its success as a port for the Americas and its shipbuilding activities. Today Glasgow is being refurbished with new buildings replacing slums, new factories and industry growing up and its finest old buildings being cleaned up and restored to their former glory.

Queen's Square, Belfast, 1897 (above). *The spacious 19th century vista of Queen's Square was doomed to disappear in the 20th century. However, the Albert Clock tower, built at Queen Victoria's command to commemorate her husband is still striking the hours. The splendid square, adjacent to Custom House Square, was near the River Laggan quaysides and was often busy with the rush and bustle that accompanies the loading and unloading of ships. Since the days of shipping, the square has lost its pre-eminence and most of its fine Victorian buildings. Plans are now afoot to put a bridge across the Laggan and a broad roadway across the square.*

Royal Avenue, Belfast, 1897 (right). *Royal Avenue runs from Donegal Square to North Street and is still a fine city street though many of the splendid buildings seen in this photograph have disappeared. The theatre in Royal Avenue has also disappeared, its place being taken rather ignominiously by a bingo hall. Another thing that was vanishing in Ireland in 1897 was the peace and stability of the city's life as evoked in this photograph. Gladstone's Irish Home rule had been rejected by the House of Lords, the Sinn Fein party was about to be born and dark clouds of a storm which would break tempestuously in 1920 were gathering.*

Princes Street, Edinburgh, 1897
(left). *From Princes Street and its continuation, Waterloo Place, can be seen the monument to Nelson on Calton Hill, a fine viewpoint over the city. There were still horse trams running up to the hill when this picture was taken and large crowds waiting to mount them. The attractions of Calton Hill, then as now, were many and included an unfinished 'Parthenon' and the City Observatory (now disused). From the hill there is a fine view across the splendid Georgian streets to the north of Princes Gardens and of the Castle Rock to the south.*

Edinburgh Castle, 1897 (right). *The imposing view of Edinburgh Castle from the Grassmarket looks today much as it did in 1897. The forbidding fortress has had an eventful life since the Picts took refuge on the crag. During medieval times the Scots and the English struggled for possession of it and in the 16th century it was held for five years by supporters of Mary, Queen of Scots, who gave birth there to the son who was to become King of England and Scotland as James I. Later, when Bonnie Prince Charlie's forces took Edinburgh in 1745 the Castle was the only part to resist him.*

Today it is a popular tourist site and the high point of the Edinburgh Festival is the spectacular Tattoo performed on the Castle's forecourt.

Darwen, Lancashire, 1895 (below). *Darwen, which lies to the south of Blackburn, is typical of the industrial towns of the north which provided Britain's wealth in the 19th century. Tall chimneys belch smoke over the green countryside and terraces of houses huddle together between the vast factory buildings which dominate the townscape like churches and cathedrals of industry.*

The neglect and poverty which were a feature of the past, have gone today and Darwen's population of some 30,000 inhabitants are better cared for than in the days of the soot-black mills which continue to produce cotton, paper and chemicals in an improved environment.

Ironbridge, Salop, 1892 (right). *In 1892 the cast-iron bridge across the River Severn near Telford had been standing only thirteen years but has remained to this day as a monument to Abraham Darby and his son. The elder Darby discovered how to smelt iron with coke, and his son, also named Abraham, carried on his father's work becoming a designer and builder of industrial structures. The bridge was one of his creations and has the peculiarity that its joints are based on those used in woodwork techniques and not on the nut and bolt systems evolved later.*

Evidence of the role of Ironbridge and nearby Coalbrookdale as the precursors of the Industrial Revolution is preserved at Bliss Hill and other local museums

War Memorial, Sheffield, 1880s (below). *The Crimean War memorial with its seated figure of Victory, erected in 1858, no longer stands at the junction of Pinstone Street and The Moor for it has been moved to the Botanical Gardens. The monument was typical of much of the public statuary which decorated British cities until two world wars and the decline of British power dampened the enthusiasm for pomp and circumstance. Monuments such as these did, however, remind people that there was pain as well as glory in the business of being a leading world power, and were a focal point for national grief, as the Cenotaph in London's Whitehall remains today.*

Quebec Street, Keighley, West Yorkshire, 1870 (above). *Quebec Street was one of the dreariest parts of Keighley's industrial district. The stream under the stone bridge ran black with polluted water and a heavy pall of smoke hung over the factories which rose over the grimy workers' cottages. Today, Keighley has been absorbed into greater Bradford and, like other industrial towns, has been much cleaned up and rebuilt. Haworth has retained its village atmosphere*

Town Hall, Liverpool, 1895 (above). *The Classical style Town Hall, built by John Wood the elder in the middle of the 18th century, was the centre of Liverpool's administration during the port's heyday. The slave, sugar, tobacco and rum trade made Liverpool rich in the 18th century. Today, the dome which once rose about the surrounding buildings is dwarfed by modern architecture, symbolising Liverpool's efforts to overcome the problems which arose after the sudden collapse of the shipping business .*

London

During the last hundred years London has more than doubled in size and most of the built-up area has developed since the turn of the century. As the industrial life of northern towns has declined so the population of London has continued to expand. New areas are being developed east of Tower Bridge, in what was once one of the world's greatest ports, and buildings, once adequate for Victorian commerce, are being replaced by sky-scraping tower blocks. The London preserved in the photographs of the 19th and early 20th century, therefore have a special poignancy as reminders of a long lost society.

Ludgate Hill and Circus, c.1890. *Evidently the traffic congestion of Ludgate Hill is not a 20th-century phenomenon, only now it is vehicles of metaphorical rather that literal horsepower that clog the streets. Due to their proximity to the Thames the environs of Ludgate Hill and Circus were a busy mercantile and trading area. Today, there are still many offices so that if one is in the area on a non-working day it seems almost deserted.*

London has always been a city in a state of transformation but the changes that have taken place since the 19th century have been more radical than at any other period in its history.

By the time of Queen Victoria's accession, the London of the landed gentry, with its riverside bordered with splendid mansions whose gardens reached down to the water's edge, had already begun to disappear under the commercial pressure evident below London Bridge, where sailing ships of all kinds jostled each other as they unloaded cargoes from the expanding Empire. By 1850 London east of the Tower had become the most important port in Britain and soon the docks of St Katharine, London, Surrey, East and West India were to be crowded with the shipping of the mightiest power on earth. The development of wharf and warehouse did not stop here, however, but crept up river along the south bank until the whole of that side of the Thames was lined with warehouses and offices, sometimes of stone or brick but also of unsightly corrugated iron.

Growth and wealth

As London became the centre of wealth and commerce, it attracted people from parts of Britain who came to work in the city where, according to legend, the streets were paved with gold. London's population, which had been less than a million in 1801, had risen to two and a half million by mid-century and by the turn of the century to over six million. The demands of the growing population caused an outward expansion of the urban area. The wealthier inhabitants moved to Belgravia and Pimlico where terraces of splendid houses, each with their own portico, were built on estates owned by the great landed families. Mayfair was developed by the Grosvenors, and the Cadogans sold part of their estate in Knightsbridge to Henry Holland who developed it with Sir Hans

Organ grinder, 1895 (below). In the Victorian era there was a proliferation of street entertainers particularly in London. Initially these were people unable to earn a living due to disability of circumstance and in the absence of any social security system they were forced to 'busk' as an alternative to begging. The prosperity of England in the mid- to late-19th century attracted immigrants to try their luck and many of the entertainers of this period came from Europe, generally Germany and Italy.

The Italians were especially associated with organ grinders, often a 'patron' or 'godfather' would own several organs and then pay between £3 and £4 to a poor family in the south of Italy to purchase their son. The boy would then be expected to work for his 'patron'.

An average barrel organ had eight tunes: a song, a waltz, a hornpipe, a polka, two dance tunes and two pieces of classical music (usually opera); the tunes were changed once a year at a cost of 10 shillings

Dancing bear 1895 (below, left). Bears had been used for entertainment in Britain for at least 200 years before this photograph was taken in 1895. Bear-baiting was a favourite sport of the Elizabethans inspiring Shakespeare with lines like: 'They have tied me to a stake; I cannot fly, But, bear-like, I must fight the course.' (Macbeth V viii)

The Victorians had a great love of novelty and a dancing bear would have had enormous appeal. They were also fascinated by the paradox of an animal acting like a human being. The popular artist Landseer used this theme time and time again in his paintings, varying the treatment from the comic and absurd (as in 'Laying Down the Law'), to the sentimental (as in 'The Well Bred Sitters...'), and occasionally to the horrific (as in 'The Cat's Paw').

Brown bears are the easiest bears to train to do tricks and are the most commonly used in circuses which were very popular in the late 19th century. In this photo the bear is evidently mimicking a soldier shouldering arms. Tricks with a military or patriotic theme were particularly popular; on the order to 'die for their country' pet animals would rollover extending their legs stiffly towards the sky.

Today, the photograph would appal any civilized eye as being documentation of a tasteless travesty. However, it is well to remember that we still keep animals in zoos, that we have a factory farming-system and that the supremely atavistic hobby of dog-fighting is on the increase to the detriment of breeds such as the Pit Bull Terrier.

Lambeth Riverside, 1870s. *This scene of ramshackle Dickensian housing on the banks of the Thames at Lambeth, is typical of the dwellings which lined the river opposite Westminster and all along the River in the 19th century. It could not have been a pleasant place to live as the water was no more than an open sewer. At this time these men could see on the far bank the new houses of Parliament rising in all its Neogothic splendour. Not far away was Lambeth Palace once the London home of Kings and then, as now, the London home of the Archbishop of Canterbury. Today, in place of these 'slums', is the St Thomas's hospital and the old Greater London Council Offices.*

Cheyne Walk, c.1860. *Cheyne Walk, which runs by the Thames to the west of the Albert Bridge, has suffered no major changes this century. However, an ambitious and important Victorian project altered the look of the road subsequent to this photograph: the building of the Chelsea Embankment, which involved the reclamation of tidal areas. Where the boats can be seen moored is now part of the road.*

The houses of Cheyne Walk have altered very little since their construction in 1718 although the Victorians did develop the neighbourhood to a certain extent. The late 19th century saw a building programme initiated by Norman Shaw that was to change the area around Cheyne Walk without destroying the existing 'Queen Anne' houses.

The 'Building News' of 1877 was certainly impressed by Shaw's work:

'Still true to its tradition, the modern architecture of Chelsea is a revival of the old classic of the 17th century...Proceeding up the river the steamboat passenger...sees an extensive row of large, newly-built red-brick houses fronting the river and recalling in their features the style of the Stuarts.'

There is still much of the fine original wrought-iron work to be seen in the gates, railings and balconies of the 17th- and 19th-century houses. Cheyne Walk was inhabited by some of the most distinguished of the Victorian literati including George Eliot, D.G. Rossetti and Swinburne and it is still a road with great prestige.

Building the Thames Embankment, c.1865.
The original two sections of the Embankment at Victoria and Chelsea have changed little since they were built.

The Victoria Embankment was the first to be constructed, from Westminster Bridge east to Blackfriars Bridge. It was begun in 1864 and completed in 1870; the same architect, Sir Joseph Bazalgette, also built the Chelsea Embankment which runs for a mile from Battersea Bridge to Chelsea Bridge. The building of the Embankments involved the reclamation of tidal areas, made stable, by walls no less than 8ft (2.25m) thick in places.

Once the Embankments were completed Building News recalls another suggestion in their issue of 1876: 'that the Thames Embankment itself should be converted into a boulevard — that it should be lined with cafés, restaurants, little paradises, white pavilions, white marble tables, coffee stalls and pretty paraphernalia of the kind'. The suggestion 'was denounced as if there had been suggested another burning of St Paul's'.

Sloane (whose daughter was married to a Cadogan). Houses were also built on land belonging to the Bishop of London to the north of Hyde Park at Holland Park, Bayswater and Notting Dale (now Notting Hill). This quarter eventually diminished in popularity and decayed, to be revived recently when the refurbished houses have regained some of their former elegance. In St John's Wood the development was more rural in character with individual houses whose gardens were surrounded with brick walls, which led the Victorians to believe that they were designed for the mistresses of rich men.

At first only the rich could afford to maintain villas outside the centre of London, in places like Twickenham, Ham and Chiswick, but the growing affluence of the middle classes and their demand for better housing created the fringe estates known as suburbia, where millions of Pooters settled to live their self-satisfied and comfortable lives. They had good reason to do so for it was a time of peace and plenty and Britain's rule over the earth seemed as steadfast as the morning star.

Suburbia

People who lived in suburbia worked in central London and required a reliable means of transport. This heralded the introduction of the commuter services which bring millions into the centre of the capital today. The building of railways into the city caused more upheaval as space was cleared for the tracks and cuttings for the first underground railway. The first trains, drawn by steam engines, ran between Farringdon and Paddington in 1860 and nearly asphyxiated all the passengers, but anything seemed better than the interminable traffic jams of slow-moving horse-buses, hansom cabs and commercial drays. By the 1890s the technique for deep tunnelling had been studied and perfected and, thanks to an American entrepreneurial millionaire, there were trains running along the Bakerloo, Northern and Piccadilly lines by the beginning of the 20th century in addition to the previously-built Central line.

Architecture

The rise of the merchant and trading classes had a conspicuous effect on the architecture of the new London. No longer was there the homogeneity of style identified with a particular class of society such as had existed in the 18th century; instead style became eclectic based on models of once powerful European states and Empires, predominantly the Roman, the Venetian, the Florentine, the Dutch and the Flemish Gothic. Many of the Imperial entrepreneurs began to donate their fabulous collections of cultural and ethnographic material to the nation, making it essential to build museums in which these treasures could be housed. The profits of the Great Exhibition, inspired by Prince Albert in Hyde Park in 1851, provided the necessary funds. Land was acquired between Kensington Gardens and Cromwell Road and one of London's most notable assembly of public buildings was erected, including the Roman Colosseum-style Albert Hall, the Romanesque-Gothic Natural History Museum and the Renaissance-Venetian Victoria and Albert Museum.

The birth of modern London

The rebuilding and expansion of London during the latter part of the 19th century was largely achieved by private enterprise and there was little control over what came down and what went up. There was also little overall responsibility for the welfare of the city as a whole. The result was that the city became a patchwork of districts of varying standards of accommodation and amenities; slums rubbed shoulders with affluent residential housing even in an area like Mayfair. There were of course

Building Tower Bridge, c.1890 *(above).* Tower *Bridge was designed by Sir Horace Jones and Sir John Wolfe Barry and built between 1886 and 1894. The bridge itself cost £800,000 and the total cost of construction, including the approaches, was £1,500,000. It is 88ft long, the central span comprising two drawbridges which can be raised to allow ships to pass through. These drawbridges weigh some 1,000 tons each and have been raised over 500,000 times since the bridge was built.*

The bridge itself has not changed since it was first constructed, although the original steam-driven pumping engines, built by Sir W.G. Armstrong for raising the central part, were replaced by an electric motor in 1977. *The original engines are still in working order in the museum under the southern approach to the bridge.*

From Tower Bridge one has a spectacular view of the buildings on either side of the river, including the impressive new Hay's Galleria, part of a mammoth development on the South Bank. The 19th century saw a proliferation of warehousing along the Thames due to its being an artery for trade. However, many of these buildings were destroyed in World War II and those that were left fell derelict in the 1960s and 70s when trade stopped. These warehouses are now popular as residences for the new rich.

Whitehall, c.1898 (below). *The predominantly 17th- and 18th-century buildings in Whitehall that house various Government offices remain intact although there have been changes around them. The Whitehall Theatre, for instance, was built by E.A. Stone in 1930, the Crown Estate Office by J. Murray in 1910 and the War Office (now part of the Ministry of Defence) by William Young in 1906.*

In 1898 Parliament Street was widened to ease the congested traffic flow, the west side of Whitehall & Parliament Street bearing the brunt of the necessary demolition. During this work Montagu House, built in 1868, was demolished and has subsequently been replaced by an office block. The east side of Whitehall is relatively unchanged but the statues now include Lord Mountbatten (1982), and Field Marshal Viscount Montgomery (1980). The most famous landmark in Whitehall was also erected well into the 20th century: the Cenotaph, dedicated to 'the Glorious Dead' and designed by Sir Edwin Lutyens, was placed where it now stands in 1920.

The photograph below shows workmen laying blocks in the road, probably during the widening, and an interesting variety of transport can be seen including an omnibus, hand-pushed carts, a dray and a coster's 'shay'.

public-spirited visionaries who saw that it was necessary to take positive action to improve the city. An American millionaire called Peabody and Baroness Burdett Coutts both contributed from their personal fortunes to improve the living and housing standards of the poor and, earlier, Edwin Chadwick had carried on a determined and relentless campaign against the overcrowding of churchyards and the slaughtering of cattle at Smithfield, and for public sewage systems.

The work of such reformers brought the needs of the expanding metropolis to public attention and in 1899 a body was established to take on responsibility for London as a whole, called the London County Council. This eventually became the Greater London Council and was dissolved in 1987, responsibility then passing to the individual metropolitan borough councils which had been formed in 1899 as a counter-weight to the London County Council.

Despite the lack of an overall plan and authority such as was exercised by Baron Haussmann in Paris under Napoleon III, London's progress has been steady and beneficial to the majority of all its population. Even the eclectic architecture has proved an asset for it has given London a distinctive atmosphere of its own in which beauty and ugliness, elegance and crassness co-exist, creating a scene of constant surprise and stimulus.

At the turn of the century the city again changed its appearance. In the Edwardian era the Knightsbridge shopping quarter was developed, Harrods was built and the Ritz Hotel gave Piccadilly a Parisian touch with its mansard roof and wrought-iron balconies. Haussmann had set the style for wide, city boulevards and, though London did not follow suit, some new avenues were opened up to allow a faster flow of traffic. One of these was Kingsway which cut through a slum area and another earlier one was Queen Victoria Street in

Park Lane, c.1890 (above and left). *Park Lane was originally called Tyburn Lane as it ran from the gallows at Tyburn Tree (now Marble Arch) to Hyde Park Corner. This association is far from the image that Park Lane conjures up today; it is renowned as one of the premier roads in London and was just as prestigious 100 years ago when it boasted such residents as Disraeli (Lord Beaconsfield) and Lady Palmerston. More recently, Lord Louis Mountbatten, later Earl Mountbatten of Burma, lived in Park Lane. However, one change that has occurred is that it is home to a large transient population as the London Hilton and the Grosvenor House Hotels in Park Lane now play host to the rich and famous.*

The London Hilton was built in 1963 by Lewis Solomon, Kaye and Partners on the site of one of the great mansions (at one time occupied by Syrie Maugham; interior decorator and daughter of Dr Barnardo) which made up the east side of Park Lane.

Rotten Row, c.1885. *Rotten Row is a stretch of sandy riding track in Hyde Park running parallel to the Carriage Row which is now a road carrying traffic through the park. The name 'Rotten Row' is thought to be a bastardization of 'Route Du Roi' and indeed if any riding track has a claim to that title it is this one.*

In the 19th century (as previously), Rotten Row was a place 'to see and to be seen'. It was there that the fashionable of London took a turn in their carriage or on horseback to make a display of their wealth and social position. In this respect times have changed; the increased pace of life and the increasingly subtle ways of displaying status mean that

Rotten Row is no longer what it was. However it is still considered prestigious to ride there and horses may be hired from nearby Bathurst Mews, although this is probably more the province of the tourist than the native.

Rotten Row was also the site of the magnificent Great Exhibition of 1851. The exhibition building designed by Sir Joseph Paxton was removed to Sydenham and recreated as the Crystal Palace (see pages 106 – 107). In 1982 Rotten Row was the tragic scene of a terrorist bomb attack by the IRA that resulted in the deaths of many horses and men of the Royal Horse Artillery.

the city. This was also the period when London became a great place of public entertainment with theatres springing up in Shaftesbury Avenue (the Globe and the Queen's) and the handsome Her Majesty's in Haymarket, musical halls (the Alhambra, Empire and Hippodrome) in Leicester Square, an area long renowned as a centre of prostitution.

Fall and rise

World War I though making a turning point in British Society had little effect on London's architecture but World War II did. Large areas of London were destroyed by the Luftwaffe, dramatically changing the capital's skyline and accelerating the architectural trends that had begun to appear just before the War. These trends had social undertones and signified the end of middle class predominance in society; from now on London was to acquire a new identity in its progress towards a classless society dominated by large impersonal corporate institutions.

The first signs of the changes were soon visible in the City of London which had suffered extensive damage from the bombardments and therefore had the most available land for new buildings. One of the largest sites was in the area between St Paul's, which miraculously avoided destruction, and Moorgate. The idea of building a great city estate which could provide both homes and entertainment took root and so the Barbican was created. It comprises blocks of flats, some high-rise towers and a cultural centre, designed in a certain grim style in keeping with its name which was derived from the Roman strongpoint that had once stood along this section of the city wall.

The area around St Paul's was also rebuilt, though the opportunity to show off Britain's greatest Renaissance church by her most celebrated architect was missed and the view of the west front was obscured by characterless office buildings.

The Alhambra, c.1890 (left). *The late 19th century saw a boom in theatres and music halls. The Alhambra, in Leicester Square, was a popular music hall where such artists as Wilkie Bard, Arthur Roberts and Vesta Tilley might be seen. The music halls catered for the taste of the lower classes with novelty acts, singing, clowning and magic; from the poster it would seem that Letty Lind who was performing at the Alhambra might do something on a trapeze.*

Also in Leicester Square were the Empire and the Leicester Lounge. Both of these premises were notorious haunts of prostitutes and became a target for moral protesters like Mrs Ormison Chant. These groups paraded outside the Empire with banners proclaiming 'Save our lands from sin', and, giving way to this pressure, the Empire agreed to screen the promenade from the auditorium. This provoked an angry reaction from a group of young men, including Winston Churchill, who stormed in and took down the partition.

The advent of the movies was the death blow to the music halls which had been faltering anyway. In 1927 the Empire closed, only 40 years after its opening. Today Leicester Square is a 'Mecca' for film-goers and the Alhambra is still catering to the popular audience as a cinema rather than a music hall.

Regent Street, c.1890 and 1950 (right and below). Laid out between 1813 and 1825 by John Nash, Regent Street was originally intended as part of a scheme to link Carlton House Terrace (where the Prince Regent's town house was) to Regent's Park a mile or two to the north. Since that time it has become a thriving street renowned for its shops.

Although there are no conspicuously 'modern' buildings in Regent Street all is not as 'regency' as it appears. All but a few fragments of Nash's Regent Street was destroyed in a great rebuilding of the road in the early 1920s. In fact only three Nash houses remain: two are hidden behind neon signs in Piccadilly Circus and one is the stucco-fronted York building. The reconstruction of Regent Street began in 1899 with the erection of a building which was then occupied by Kodak Ltd, but the bulk of the changes came

after World War I. By 1923 the curved section of Regent Street had been redesigned by Sir Reginald Blomfield whose six-storey buildings effected no radical change in style from Nash's original five-storey buildings. Regent Street, as we know it today, is really a product of the work done in the 1920s. In 1921 the Dickins & Jones department store was built and 1922 saw the arrival of Peter Robinson, Liberty and several others. After 1924 a major change in the Piccadilly Circus end of Regent Street took place with the demolition of the west side Quadrant which was designed in John Nash's time.

Not only did the buildings alter but the shops occupying the premises in the 19th century have nearly all disappeared. The expiration of Crown leases between 1913 and 1923 combined with the expense of the rebuilding made it impossible for many of the original firms to stay in business. Many went into receivership and some were forced to relocate to areas where the rents were cheaper.

There has been no great change to Regent Street since this picture was taken in the 1950s. Perhaps the traffic has got a little heavier and the tourists more numerous, but the architecture is still the same if somewhat cleaner.

widening of the Charing Cross Road and a roundabout to alleviate the traffic problems. However, a change in the one-way systems made a roundabout unnecessary.

The Oxford Music Hall was a popular feature of St Giles Circus 100 years ago and it remained so until after World War I when it was pulled down to make way for Lyons' tea rooms. There has been less architectural change than one might expect, although one of the original shops in Frith's photograph remains. One of the last bastions of Victoriana was the Horseshoe just to the north of St Giles Circus; initially a hotel, then a pub, it is currently being redeveloped possibly into a fast-food restaurant. North of St Giles Circus at the beginning of Tottenham Court Road, changes have been drastic.

St Giles Circus, c.1910 (above and right). *St Giles Circus has always had a traffic flow problem. It is situated at a crucial junction in the West End and efforts to overcome the congestion at this point have led to a major rebuilding on the south-east side. In 1965 one of the new London landmarks was completed by Richard Seifert & Partners: Centre Point, a sky scraper, 33 storeys, 350 ft high. It was initially designed to incorporate a*

Piccadilly Circus, c.1890 and 1960s (above and right). *At the moment Piccadilly Circus looks like a building site as it is being redesigned to improve traffic flow and pedestrian safety. Since the advent of the internal combustion engine it has become increasingly busy and perilous for pedestrians, although this photograph shows just how chaotic the traffic was a century ago.*

Despite the changes that are currently taking place in Piccadilly Circus there are also signs of the prevailing nostalgic trend in building. The London pavilion seen in this photograph is being restored to its former glory although the fine wrought-iron and glass portico is probably lost forever. Opposite the pavilion is the famous Criterion Long Bar mentioned in the Sherlock Holmes story, A Study in Scarlet; *the interior of this building has been restored since the discovery of a virtually intact fin-de-siecle decor under the 1960s plaster board facia.*

The striking thing about this early photograph is

the absence of 'Eros', the Shaftsbury Memorial. Designed by Sir Alfred Gilbert the figure is a cast in aluminium of a winged archer and his bow, intended to represent the Angel of Christian charity but more popularly known as 'Eros' (the Greek God of Love). It was erected in 1893, three years after this photograph was taken, to the Seventh Earl of Shaftesbury, an eminent philanthropist.

Across the river on the South Bank a happier transformation took place when Festival Hall was built on the site of the impressive exhibition celebrating the new age towards which Britain was moving in the post-war period. Gradually, other buildings for the arts, were added to the complex which is still in the process of evolution as new designs to improve the drab concrete facades are studied and decided upon.

Modern London

More recently, one of the most far-reaching events in the story of London was the closure of the Port of London. This took place over several years as container ships gradually took over cargoes from conventional steamers and new, larger more adequate port facilities were developed many miles down river at Tilbury.

This move eliminated one of the most picturesque quarters of London. The East End had always been the haven of the refugee populations of Europe. The Huguenots had found refuge there at the time of the religious wars in France and Jewish people had found asylum there from persecution in other countries. In the 19th century the growth of Empire trade had brought people from all over the world to London. The ethnic communities made particular parts of the East End their own. Whitechapel was a centre of the Jewish community and the Sunday markets that operate in this area have become one of London's major tourist attractions. The Chinese made Limehouse their district and gave rise to a whole mythology of this exotic corner of the metropolis. Today all that world is gone and in the derelict acres new housing is springing up beside new industry. Newspapers have deserted Fleet Street in favour of Wapping and the Isle of Dogs.

The new projects that are afoot east of Tower Bridge include developments of office blocks, skyscrapers, residential quarters, marinas, entertainment complexes and shopping precincts. A whole new city is being born down river towards Greenwich, once the home of Tudor and Stuart kings. The new style is already evident in the City where skyscrapers like those of the Westminster Bank and the P & O building are shooting up like parodies of the towers of the merchant princes of the Italian city states. Much of the architecture is undistinguished, lacking the panache of New York or the new La Reserve quarter of Paris.

Perhaps this is due to the watershed situation of the British people who view their glorious past with a certain distrust but are not entirely persuaded by the heralds of the future. The destiny of Piccadilly Circus is a case in point; for more than a decade its new face has hung in the balance appearing at times as a vision of some Hollywood space city and at others as a museum of the past. At present some kind of compromise seems to be on the way. The dominant facades of the Pavilion Theatre and the Criterion have been restored, and the statue of Eros cleaned, repaired and reinstated. The Pavilion was reopened in July 1988 after being completely rebuilt inside and divided into shops.

The fate of Piccadilly Circus reflects the change of attitude in architects and planners who only a few years ago were only too eager to demolish the buildings of Victorian London and raise in their place the indifferent creations representing the new classless society of the post-war decades. Since that period, which saw so much destruction all over Britain, an awareness of people's need for a continuing thread in their environment and their lives has begun to prevail.

The result of all this activity will, one hopes, be in character with the rest of London, a city which represents the short-sightedness and vision, the self-interest and idealism, and the fundamental love of its citizens for their capital. □

The Strand, c.1895 (below). The Strand has always been a busy thoroughfare carrying much of London's east-west traffic. Consequently, a major change in the appearance of the road since Frith's photograph is that it has been widened to accommodate more vehicles. The eastern end of the Strand was so narrow that there was barely room for three lanes of traffic and the pavement was so unaccommodating that on a wet day pedestrians would get mud splattered. Harold Clunn in his book London Rebuilt 1897–1927 even recalls the meat hanging outside a butcher's shop regularly getting splashed as carriages and omnibuses went by.

The widening of the eastern end of the Strand was begun in 1899 and was completed, after the delays caused by World War I, c.1924. The shops which had filled the north side were demolished to allow the road to be widened to its present 100ft (30m) width. Last of these buildings to go was the Coach and Horses hotel which was pulled down in 1923 with plans to enlarge the new building of Bush House which now occupies the island site at the eastern end of the Strand.

Three years after the death of Queen Victoria, in 1904, most of the new building were completed on the south side of the Strand and by 1922 it could be said that the road was looking very much as it does today with familiar landmarks like the rather imposing Australia House, built in 1911–18 on the site of the old Olympic Theatre by A. Marshall Mackenzie and A.G.R. Mackenzie.

Charing Cross Station, c.1895. *Few changes have been made to the west end of the Strand; the Charing Cross Hotel on the right of the photograph is still standing, set back from the road, a magnificent Victorian Gothic superstructure over the station. Built in 1864 for the South Eastern Railway Company by Sir John Hawkshaw, the station is still a key mainline terminal and is additionally linked to the underground network. The hotel was designed by E.M. Barry and opened in 1865; it was, and still is, one of the best hotels in the West End. Barry also designed the Eleanor Cross in the station forecourt, a memorial of the original cross which gave the place its name.*

In the late 19th century the Strand was renowned for its fine restaurants such as

Gatti's, Royal Adelaide, Pratti's, Romano's, the Fountain, the Golden Cross, and many others – of these only Simpson's and the Savoy remain. There are fewer theatres too; Tivoli's Music Hall, the Gaiety and the Olympic are no more but the Savoy, which opened in 1881 with Patience *by Gilbert and Sullivan still stands, as do the Adelphi, the Strand, the Vaudeville and the Lyceum (now a disco).*

The hansom cab that is so evident in Frith's photograph continued to be used up to the World War II; one can be seen evidently leaving the station, loaded up with luggage and a bicycle. They were named after Joseph Hansom (1803–82), an architect who, in 1834, patented a 'suspended axle' for a cabriolet.

The Sir Paul Pindar, c.1880 (above and right). *The Sir Paul Pindar in Bishopsgate was named after the merchant who first built a house and shop on the site. Sir Paul Pindar built the house in 1620 and in the 18th century it became a tavern called the Paul Pindar Head. It remained a pub until 1890 when it was demolished by the Great Eastern Railway. The carved oak facade, dating back to the 17th century, is now behind the gift-shop inside the Victoria and Albert Museum! (Shown here on the right.) There is still a pub called the Sir Paul Pinder (sic) in Bishopsgate.*

Like much of the city there is a mixture of architectural styles in this area ranging from the 16th- and 17th- to the 20th-century. For instance the church of St Bartolph Bishopsgate rebuilt in 1725 is dwarfed by its proximity to the Hong Kong Bank built in 1975 by Ley Colebeck and Partners and Richard Seifert and Partners, which stands an overpowering 300 ft (100 metres) high.

London Law Courts, c.1890 (right). *Opened in 1882 the Law Courts (officially the Royal Courts of Justice) in the Strand replaced the congested and inconvenient courts, described by Dickens in* Bleak House, *that used to be held in Westminster Hall. The building was begun by G.E. Street RA, and finished by his son, A.E. Street, and Sir Arthur Bloomfield; the courts are constructed of brick faced with stone and the characteristically ornate 'Gothic' exterior has altered very little since it was extended in 1911–13.*

Opposite the main entrance to the Law Courts is the tiny shop of Twinings, the tea merchants, and further along can be seen the Temple Bar memorial. It was designed by J.E. Boehm and set up in 1880. It comprises two statues of Queen Victoria and Edward VII (then Prince of Wales) which flank a bronze 'griffin' (designed by C.B. Birch). The monument denotes the end of the Strand and the beginning of Fleet Street as well as the boundary between Westminster and the City.

Jubilee 1897

On June 22, 1897 Queen Victoria's Diamond Jubilee was celebrated, when she rode through the City of London to a Thanksgiving at St Pauls Cathedral. It was an occasion for extraordinary demonstrations of patriotic fervour. During Victoria's reign Britain had struggled through the worst phase of the Industrial Revolution, world trade had increased as the Empire grew larger and a vast new strata of middle-class society which had come to have a major influence on national life had come into being.

Though the Queen had been much criticised for her retirement from public life after the death of her husband Prince Albert, all was forgiven and forgotten at her Jubilee which marked the summit of British success and power and awoke in all the population, rich and poor, a patriotic pride which has never been equalled.

Park Lane, Jubilee Arch (left). *In 1896 the Duke of Westminster began a rebuilding programme for the area around Park Lane. Both the Dukes of Bedford and Westminster had decided to take advantage of expiring leases to redevelop and improve those areas of London that they owned. By the Jubilee year the job was well underway and to add to the festivities a Jubilee Arch was built.*

The Queen arrives at St Pauls. *Like Park Lane all London was decorated for the Jubilee and street festivals abounded. Below we can see the Queen arriving in her royal landau at the steps of St Pauls, which are crowded with loyal citizens, none of whom has the slightest doubt about the glory of their sovereign and their Empire. The Thanksgiving was held on the steps of the building since the Queen was felt to be too infirm to enter.*

Preparations for the great day
(left). *All over London decorations and bunting were brought out to festoon every building and every house. In Queen Victoria Street which was built in 1871 as part of a plan to create major thoroughfares that would facilitate the flow of traffic around London, a gentleman with the news-sheet proclaims the forthcoming celebrations as the busy life of the city goes on around him.*

This whole area of London was completely changed from 1870 to 1890. Roads were created or widened and Victoria Street was created to link Victoria Station with Westminster Abbey, Whitehall and Charing Cross. Although in 1897 the facades of Queen Victoria Street were only 26 years old, they were already grey with dirt. Victorian London was notoriously sooty and it was this rather than aesthetic whim that turned the most popular building material from stone to red brick.

It was not just in London that celebrations were held, after all there had never been a Dimond Jubilee before. Throughout the Empire the fireworks exploded and toasts were drunk, gifts were sent – the Cape Colony sent a battleship – and money raised in the Queens name for hospitals and homes. There was an outporing of gratitude to their Monarch of sixty years who ruled over half the globe.

The procession crossing Westminster Bridge. *The procession was on scale that matched the occasion. Soldiers of the Empire marched before the landau, with a guard of honour made up of 22 Indian Cavalry officers rode alongside. Forty-two foreign princes rode in the wake of the Queen lead by Captain Ames of the Life Guards – the tallest man in the army at 6 feet 8 inches. Spectators paid up to two guineas a ticket for a seat on the route.*

The view of London from Westminster Bridge has altered little from the great day. Though somewhat more from the time when Wordsworth wrote of 'ships, towers, domes, theatres, and temples lie Open unto the fields..' ('Upon Westminster Bridge' 1802). Since 1897 there have been various changes to this scene: County Hall was built in 1912-22, the Millbank Tower in 1963, the Shell Building in 1957-62, the Royal Festival Hall in 1951 and the rest of the South Bank arts complex which was completed with the opening of the new National Theatre in 1976.

St Paul's from the River, c.1880 (left). *There have been quite startling changes in this skyline with the advent of high-rise buildings. Whilst St Paul's was once the highest building for many miles it is now clustered round with tower blocks which stand like so many upturned bricks — a monument to the growth in population and increased pressure on architects to go up since they can't spread out. Nevertheless, a panoramic view is still possible for those strong in wind and limb from the viewing gallery at the top. The warehouses in the foreground of the photograph remind one of the reason for the number of offices near St Paul's: its proximity to the Thames made it an obvious choice particularly for import and export companies. Much of the warehousing was destroyed during World War II War and, since the Thames is no longer the artery for trade it once was, it was not rebuilt. Those warehouses that remain are now being converted into private dwellings, highlighting the prevailing trend in building to adapt rather than destroy.*

St Paul's after the Blitz (above, right). *St Paul's narrowly escaped destruction on the night of 29 December 1940 when the Luftwaffe made one of its heaviest raids on London. Among the hail of bombs there were 10,000 incendiaries which set alight the buildings around Wren's masterpiece. A photographer immortalised the potent image of the cathedral still standing after the flames and smoke had subsided.*

The development of Paternoster Square (right). *Much of the architecture surrounding St Pauls has changed radically since the bombing. Paternoster Square a quarter to the south which had traditionally been an area of booksellers and publishers — Dr. Johnson's Grub Street — was redeveloped with towers of glass and concrete completely out of character with Wren's masterpiece.*

Southwark, 1897 (left). *The Borough has changed little since the 19th century; surprisingly, it has retained much of its character despite its position close to the Thames, London Bridge and London Bridge Station. Opened in 1836 Borough is the oldest surviving underground station in London.*

One of the main commercial buildings in Southwark was the Hop Exchange built in the reigns of Charles II and Queen Anne and rebuilt by R.H. Moore in 1866 as Central Buildings. It is still in use as a centre of the hop industry.

In 1905 the diocese of Southwark was created and the church of St Saviour and St Mary Overy became Southwark Cathedral. Although it has been repaired and altered, the Cathedral remains one of the finest examples of Gothic architecture in London.

Kensington High Street, c.1899 (below, left). *Kensington was not properly absorbed into London until the mid- to late 19th century; with the expansion of the capital came an increasing pressure upon the hitherto quiet roads and it was this that was responsible for a great amount of rebuilding around the High Street.*

Changes had begun as early as 1892 when the houses abutting the High Street were demolished to make way for a row of shops and a block of flats (Iverna Court 1893-1903). In 1902 the London County Council decided to widen the High Street to accommodate the growing demands of traffic. To effect this widening all the buildings on the north side of the road were demolished between Church Street (including the Civet Cat) and Palace Gardens. The Civet Cat was rebuilt but a large portion of the new frontage was taken up by Barker's, whose grand shop was completed in 1904. A fire in 1912 caused Barker's to rebuild their damaged store but it has remained in its 1912 manifestation and to this day dominates that section of the High Street.

Elephant and Castle, c.1890 (right). *There has been an Elephant and Castle public house at the Elephant and Castle from before the 16th century. The area derives its name from the pub and the pub's name is suspected of being the result of a witty mispronunciation of Eleanor of Castile. The shapes and styles may have changed but there is still an Elephant and Castle at the Elephant and Castle. The cabling that is joined on the roof of the pub in Frith's photograph is now piped underground, and of course the cobbles have been replaced with tarmacadam.*

The area around the Elephant and Castle was substantially rebuilt in 1960-65 as part of a new plan to simplify the road system by linking two roundabouts with a broad carriageway; were it not for the pub it would not now be easy to recognize the road from the 19th-century photograph. One interesting point to note is the sign of a distinctly modern trend already beginning in Victorian London: the building backing on to the pub is a vegetarian restaurant.

A day out at Crystal Palace

The Crystal Palace was originally built by Sir Joseph Paxton for the Great Exhibition of 1851 in Hyde Park, near Rotten Row, but was subsequently relocated. Later in 1851 the clock which had adorned the Hyde Park Palace was removed to King's Cross Station where it can still be seen. In 1854 the entire structure was removed to a permanent home in Sydenham; in 1920 it became the home of the Imperial War Museum. The museum moved in 1935 to the Bethlem Royal Hospital building which it still occupies.

Only a year after the Imperial War Museum moved the Crystal Palace largely was destroyed by fire. The only remaining parts were the two towers which were demolished in 1940 in the interests of national security as they were landmarks for enemy aircraft. In 1958 the BBC erected a television mast on the site, and in 1964 the international sports complex was opened.

The conflagration, 1936 (above). *The end came for The Crystal Palace in December 1936. The building had been neglected for some time, even though it was still a favourite place for Londoners to visit at the weekends. The flames could be seen from miles around, and hundreds of people were evacuated.*

An Outing to Sydenham 1890s (below). Crystal Palace has long been a place for leisure activities, its grounds making the perfect setting for a day out. Its size made it possible for Crystal Palace to be host to various sports and events including the popular spectacle of ballooning.

Although the Palace itself was destroyed in 1936, a sports complex designed by Sir Hubert Bennett was opened in 1964 that ensures the continuance of sport at Crystal Palace. The grounds are still much used for leisure outings, particularly for children. The park includes a children's zoo, a boating lake, and sculptures and a collection of strange 'prehistoric' animals in bronze, relics from the 1851 Exhibition which are set up in a prehistoric setting.

Changes in fashion mean that full-length skirts and bowler hats are no longer, but the crowds still gather to watch the athletics or simply to enjoy a stroll in the open space.

One of the enduring delights of today's Crystal Palace, are the summer concerts. Picknickers lay out their suppers on the grass of the natural theatre overlooking the lake and watch the sunset die as the orchestra is lit up by fireworks.

Crystal Palace today. The only visible reminder of the great palace of crystal that was once the star attraction of Sydenham are the great foundations, urns, statues and lions which graced the glittering halls.

Earls Court Station, 1878 (below). Anyone standing on Earls Court Metropolitan railway station today would find the scene little changed from the one in this photograph. The gas lamps may have gone, but the booking office and stairs to the platforms remain. Today, of course, the trains are no longer drawn by steam engines, but the carriages are of the same broad construction which seems more appropriate to a normal railway than an underground system. The Metropolitan ran in a cutting just below the surface of the city. Later, in 1884, underground transport was improved by the invention of techniques for building deep tunnels, making the modern 'tube' underground possible.

Paddington, 1911 (right). The arrival of the boat train at Paddington was a special occasion. Hackney carriages gathered to collect the ocean liner passengers and their luggage, some of which would have been registered to Paddington and collected from the special enclosure on the platform. Station guards and porters bustled about, while friends and relations waited anxiously looking for those they had come to meet. The day of boat trains has gone, but Paddington is busier than ever with inter-city trains to Penzance and Cardiff, and the morning and evening rush of commuters and shoppers. The main structure of the station has changed little since 1911, though further platforms have been added.

Omnibus, Oxford Street, c.1910 (above). The horse-drawn omnibus replaced the cramped carriage named after George Shillibeer who had established the first public transportation service in London.

The horse-drawn coach, seen here in Oxford Street, was a much more comfortable affair. It had proper rows of seats upstairs and side screens that would conceal ladies' legs from the eyes of pedestrians below. These omnibuses were also the harbingers of the street advertising which clamours for the public's attention today. This one is promoting the teas of Sir Thomas Lipton, a self-made man who became a millionaire, but whom Edwardian society disparagingly referred to as 'the grocer'.

London Docks, c.1880 (left). The London Docks lay in Wapping immediately below Tower bridge and the Pool of London where steamers moored along the banks of the river. This was the oldest and in many ways the most colourful part of dockland with old riverside pubs like The Prospect of Whitby, which is now a tourist attraction, and Execution Dock where pirates and other lawbreakers of the high seas were hanged.

The Royal Albert Dock, 1950s (below). The Royal Docks were the furthest down river of all the London docks and comprised the Victoria, opened in 1855; the Royal Albert (1880) and King George V (1921) Docks. The Royal Albert covered 230 acres and was the largest expanse of artificially enclosed water in the world.

There are no cargo steamers in the Royal Albert Dock today but the stretch of water is still there converted into a marina where the pleasure boats of those who live in the surrounding new estate are moored.

West India Docks c.1880 (left). The West India docks on the Isle of Dogs were opened in 1802 to specifically handle the lucrative Caribbean trade of timber, fruit, grain and spices. It was near here at Millwall that Isambard Kingdom Brunel built his huge Great Eastern paddle-steamer in 1858 hoping to dominate the great transatlantic shipping business.

The cargo ships that once filled the docks have now been replaced by container ships whose boxed cargoes wait for them down river at Tilbury and the Isle of Dogs has become a building site where a new London is being created with homes for the city's workers and offices for businesses including such institutions as The Daily Telegraph.

Upper Norwood, c.1895. *A train from London Bridge would take you to Norwood, a fashionable suburb of London inhabited by that typically Victorian 'upper middle' class. Suburban areas like Norwood and Sydenham grew up around wells or spas where the London gentry could go to 'take the water'; some of these wells were medicinal, some sacred but now they exist only in names such as Tunbridge Wells. The advances made in analytical chemistry in the last century made these spas and their 'hydropathic establishments' obsolete but not before the spores of London had taken root.*

A century ago Norwood was inhabited by well-to-do merchants, senior civil servants, city businessmen, retired army officers and the like — a class whose life-style was the epitome of a respectable Victorian family. At that time many large houses were built, often in the Victorian Osborne, Italianate style; nowadays, most of these large houses have been demolished or converted into flats and a similar fate has befallen the hotels and 'hydropathic establishments' although some, like The Queen's Head in Upper Norwood, have survived as hotels.

Hampstead High Street, 1898 (right). Architecturally, very little has changed in Hampstead since this photograph was taken. There are now traffic lights at the junction with Heath Street, and Hampstead underground, the deepest in London, was built on the right-hand corner site in 1907. A little further down the High Street, a site that used to be a garage, has been developed to provide a number of small modern houses and some new shops. Very few of the shops in Hampstead today can claim to have been there for nine, let alone ninety years; high rates and rents account for this as well as for the increased numbers of estate agents and building societies.

Hampstead has retained nevertheless some of its village atmosphere despite a large migrating population that throngs the streets in the evening having travelled in from further up the Northern Line. The village is still popular with the arty community although only the most commercially successful actors, artists and writers can afford to live there. Once the home to the likes of Keats, Constable, and D.H. Lawrence, Hampstead is becoming increasingly the province of the wealthy rather than the talented.

Putney High Street, 1887 (right). This photograph was taken just a year after the construction of Putney Bridge by Sir Joseph Bazalgette, who also designed the Victoria and Chelsea Embankments. The Thames had clearly flooded; nowadays, the threat of flood has been significantly reduced by the building of the Thames Flood Barrier which was completed in 1982. The Barrier lies across the Thames at Woolwich. It was designed by Rendel, Palmer and Tritton and took eight years to build.

To the north of Putney Bridge is All Saints Church built in 1874 by G.E. Street. It boasts, among other things, stained glass by Burne-Jones and William Morris. The church on the south side is St Mary's which was rebuilt in 1835 except for the 15th-century tower which was subsequently rebuilt in 1982 after a fire.

Putney has long been associated with rowing; the Oxford and Cambridge boat race has started there since 1845, the course ending at Mortlake, to the west.

A Sense of History

The castles, abbeys and country houses that provide pleasure and interest to travellers about the British countryside are the visible evidence of the struggle to attain our present level of civilisation. In these mansions of power, barons bishops and powerful courtiers, the squirearchy and the merchants have held sway; creating centres of power where with friends and allies they could plan their strategies, raise their families and enjoy their leisure in secure havens of peace.

Tintern Abbey, Gwent, c.1870. It was the so-called 'Lake Poets' who first made lovely Tintern Abbey fashionable. Samuel Coleridge and William Wordsworth visited it on tours along the River Wye in the late 18th century, and both enthused over its rural and architectural perfection. Next the artists arrived — amongst them J.M.W. Turner — who sketched idyllic views of the Abbey and then published their copper-engravings back in London, Bristol and Birmingham. By the time this photograph was taken, the Abbey and its glorious position were familiar sights, whether or not one had actually visited them.

Tintern still typifies to modern eyes the essentially English scene of an 'olde worlde' village with its noble, soaring ruin on the river bank: the view from the Wye is almost the same. Only the river itself has changed, for now we are more likely to see splashing canoes or puttering launches on the water than the old working-boats of the photograph.

The castles, abbeys and historic mansions that are scattered throughout the British countryside are more than picturesque elements of the rural scene: they reveal much of the history of Britain. Some are now gaunt ruins, others display well-maintained facades, but they were all the power-houses of their age and those who lived in them had the ability to dramatically influence and shape national life.

When the Normans came to England in the wake of William the Conqueror's victory at Battle in 1066, they brought with them a disciplined concept of government that was to lay the foundations of a new national society. William gave his lords land and they repaid him with loyalty and the control of the subject peoples over whom they ruled. The castle was their power house, the first elementary moat and bailey buildings the foundations of which are still visible as mounds and ditches, but later strongly fortified keeps, such as Cliffords' Tower at York.

The Norman castles became fortresses, their owners ruling over vast feudal estates, providing armed men for the king and protection for the farmers and peasants who lived and worked in their shadow. Arundel in Sussex was one such castle, built by Roger Montgomery soon after the Norman Conquest; another was the one built by the Berry Pomeroy family in Devon and yet another was the castle which Robert de Romille built at Skipton.

The idea of rule through such strongpoints was developed by the Plantagenet kings in their efforts to subdue the other countries then forming part of the British Isles. Edward I built several castles in Wales, notably at Caernarvon where he presented his son to the recalcitrant Welsh as their first Prince of Wales, a title that has been held by the heir to the English throne ever since right up to the present Charles Prince of Wales.

Brambletye, Kent, 1890 and 1931 (left and below). These 'before and after' views of the delicate East Sussex ruins of Brambletye illustrate perfectly how attitudes changed towards Britain's architectural heritage during the intervening 40 years. It is not that the Victorians did not appreciate their ancient buildings (and 1631, when Brambletye was built, was quite ancient enough); it is just that to them, the perfect way to view a ruin was to see it as part of the landscape, in its noble and natural state, as old as the surrounding countryside.

By the 1930s, all this seemed far too sentimental. A modern age had dawned, of style and energy, and an ivy-covered hump was no good to anyone. So all over the country, led by the Ministry of Public Buildings and Works (later the Department of the Environment and now English Heritage), buildings such as this were carefully stripped of their unflattering greenery and restored as closely as possible to their original state — much as we see Brambletye today.

Rochester Castle, Kent 1890 (left). The Norman Castle at Rochester was the Victorians' view of the perfect castle: ancient — the keep was built in about 1127 — overgrown and steeped in legend. The castle was built by the Archbishop of Canterbury, William de Corbeil, who was given the castle by Henry I. It is a luxurious (for the time) and massive building, four storeys high with a magnificent great hall. In 1215 the castle was laid to seige by King John, whose men dug a tunnel under the south tower and brought it tumbling down. The tower was rebuilt by Henry III in the then popular round form.

In 1890 the castle had been decaying for some 500 years and was in just the elegaic state that was popular at the time. Today, the castle is restored and is open to the public, clean and polished with tour guides and printed histories, just the place for a day out with the children.

Bolton Abbey, North Yorkshire, c.1870. (above). *It was no uncommon sight at the time this photograph was taken to see a well brought-up young lady at her easel out in the countryside. After all, the ability to sketch and paint in water-colours was considered an essential part of her education: an accomplishment, like piano-playing, fine stitchery and perhaps a little French, to be highly prized. First a private tutor would be engaged, and a chaperone provided, and then off they would go in search of the picturesque. And what better setting could they find than Bolton Abbey, described by John Ruskin himself as 'more beautifully situated than any other ruin in this country'.*

Bolton Abbey is in fact the name of the North Yorkshire village built around the remains of the Augustinian Priory seen in the background. It nestles peacefully on the generous banks of the River Wharfe, surrounded by woods and hills: the perfect rural retreat. Thanks to the architect G.E. Street, the nave of the Priory was re-roofed and restored between 1875 and 1880, and now serves as the tiny village's magnificent and unique parish church.

Conway Castle, Gwynedd, 1913 (right). *The summer before the year of the outbreak of World War II was said to be one of the most sublime there ever was. The days were long and balmy and there was nothing to do but enjoy the weather. Those lucky enough to own a car might well have spent the summer on a motoring holiday in Wales – a fashionable pastime – and if they visited Conway (or, more properly, Conwy), they were sure to be entranced by the Castle there. It had been a favourite of the Victorians – 'there is no spot which the artist will at first sight view with greater rapture, or quit with greater reluctance' enthused one guidebook – and in 1913, with its eight ivy-clad 'drum' towers and views over the town and the sea, it was the perfect place for a motor-party to stop for 'tiffin', or a picnic lunch.*

The ivy has been torn down now, revealing an even more impressive sight than before: huge, smooth ramparts standing sentinel over what are no longer the relaxed and spacious streets of the photograph, but a bustling, colourful seaside resort. The summers seem shorter now, too.

Threat to royal supremacy

As the barons grew in strength they sometimes challenged the authority of the king, creating great centres of power such as that of the Percy family in the north-east at Alnwick. Others fought each other as they lined up behind one potential king or another, like the Lancastrians and Yorkists during the Wars of the Roses.

With the Tudors snatching the throne from the last Yorkist, Richard III, the monarchy was firmly established and the powers of the great magnates diminished. The peace of Tudor times encouraged the building of a new type of great house: no longer fortresses but imposing country manors with large windows instead of the narrow arrow slits and wrought-iron gates in place of a defensive portcullis and drawbridge.

If the Norman and Plantagenet kings used the nobility to bring administrative order to England, they also worked in alliance with the church, whose bishops and abbots, who ruled vast estates from their abbeys and monasteries, were as powerful as the barons.

Church estates grew prodigiously in size and importance, until they threatened the king's supremacy, resulting in a headlong clash which reached a crisis in the reign of Henry VIII. He dis-solved the monasteries, giving their lands and buildings to sympathetic noblemen. Many monasteries, such as Fountains Abbey, Rievaulx and Glastonbury, were allowed to crumble away through the centuries into picturesque, ivy-covered ruins; others like Lacock Abbey and Woburn Abbey became country mansions.

The rise of the merchant classes, growing rich and more influential as the Elizabethan empire expanded overseas, challenging that of the Spanish Hapsburgs, brought another change to Britain and the power of the monarchy. They exercised their 'middle class' power in Parliament and soon crossed swords with the Royalists, gradually diminishing monarchial power and finally executing Charles I.

The Romantic Age

The new ruling class thrived under the restored monarchy of Charles II and their life-style created a new London and a new countryside in which the architecture was elegant and classical. Thus developed the Age of Reason and the age of the country house. People of that period were more concerned with the present than with the past and the ruined castles and crumbling abbeys were left to moulder a condition which appealed to the Romantic Age that followed.

The pioneers of Romanticism – Wordsworth, Coleridge, Keats and Byron – revelled in decaying buildings and ivy-covered walls which, like mountains and lakes, waterfalls and grottoes, embodied the mysteries of nature. At a time when the smoke and clangour of industry were beginning to dominate towns and spread out into the countryside, the natural life appeared particularly seductive. Throughout the 19th century, ruined castles were popular settings for romantic novels. Authors such as Horace Walpole set the fashion in the 18th century with novels like *The Castle of Otranto*, and Sir Walter Scott later had everyone bewitched by his vision of the past.

Love of the picturesque

In the Victorian age, when Francis Frith began his long journeys around Britain with his heavy camera, the love of the picturesque was at its height. The harsh reality of medieval life was totally ignored and in its place there grew a notion of a mythical time when knights were bold and gallant and fair ladies were meek and pure. This concept of the past, like the modern cinema screen, was a

Castle Gateway, Berry Pomeroy, Devon, 1890 (above). *As long as a castle was in a pretty place, as long as it was covered in luxuriant ivy and, most of all, as long as it was ruined, the 1890 connoisseur of British castles was happy. Berry Pomeroy satisfied all those conditions: it was built on a rock overlooking a tributary of the River Dart in Devon, surrounded by greenery and the sound of babbling water. It was by then almost completely smothered in climbing plants, and definitely a ruin: little more remained of the place than the photograph shows here.*

Today's visitor to Berry Pomeroy and other such noble piles is looking more for historical facts than sentimental effects, however. The dangerously clinging ivy has been cleared away to show the buildings' bones and the tourists who troop around the ruins now are taught all about its 13th-century foundations, its addition (to the right of the picture) of a fine 16th-century mansion, and its eventual destruction during the Civil Wars of 1642-49.

Corfe Castle, Dorset, 1890 (right). *Corfe Castle was once one of the country's most enviable fortresses – King John's favourite castle, it is said – and for over four hundred years its massive walls dominated the little Dorset village that takes its name. During the Civil Wars it was almost razed to the ground, but it is still the focal point of the village, standing brave and gaunt on the horizon. Even without the patronage of the Castle and its inhabitants, the village prospered until in 1890, when this photograph was taken, it could boast a wide (though lamentably stony) main street, a handsome clock-towered church, and even an impressive shop-front designed in the latest fashion. It relied on the outlying farms for its produce, here being drawn in on one of the huge boat-wagons of the day, and on agriculture and local industries such as clay-mining for its prosperity.*

The ruin is now in the care of English Heritage and is one of the most picturesque survivors of Hardy's Wessex.

The Victorian Country House

The social life of the more affluent upper classes of the 19th century often revolved around country house parties. These gatherings provided an opportunity for discreet business deals between the men, gossip among the women, and flirtation for their young sons and daughters. As well as providing copious meals, the host and hostess of a country house kept their guests amused by organising shooting and fishing parties, in season, and to fill in odd moments there were garden games such as tennis, bowls, skittles and, of course, croquet.

Erdigg Park, Wrexham, 1909 (above). *Here at Erdigg Park, which was built by the son of a surveyor of the British navy in 1682 and passed by marriage to Simon York in the 18th century, the guests in their varied headgear, have been specially posed by the photographer for an artistic picture.*

Broughton House near Banbury, 1898 (left). *The formal walled garden at Broughton House provided a pleasant and sheltered spot for a moment's relaxation in the sunshine. The story of Broughton House is in many ways typical of that of many country houses which have survived the upsets of Britain's political history and the ill fortunes of their owners. In the 18th century, Thomas Twistleton became the owner through marriage and in the 19th the house was extensively repaired by George Gilbert Scott. More recently, in 1955, the splendid mansion has been restored thanks to Lord Sayle and Sele and funds from the Historic buildings council.*

**Hall Barn, Buckinghamshire
1898** (below). *Edmund Waller, the poet,
after his return from exile in France, built
Hall Barn while his memories of the Palace
of Versailles were still strong. Though the
building did not try to emulate the grandeur of the French palace it had certain
features which were fashionable at the
French court. The static water needed
constant attention to prevent a take over
by weeds and lilies, and the lawns were
always in need of mowing and sweeping
to preserve their well groomed appearance.*

Hopetoun House, Lothian, 1880
(right). *A great deal of the social high life
of Victorian time took place in country
houses. Hopetoun House was famous for
its house parties. Here, among many, we
have the Prince of Wales, later Edward
VII (in the centre of the picture), Princess
Alexandra and their son, later to become
George V. Parties such as these were the
means by which high society maintained
its position and protected its privileges.*

squalor, drunkenness and brutality were rife, and which had been exposed by writers like Charles Dickens, it was necessary to have a palliative.

History is what people like to make it and in the late Victorian age the history of Britain was rewritten in the spirit of the ruined buildings, their outlines softened by the vegetation that grew over them and their dour reality coloured by the pageantry of the imagination.

Refurbishment of ancestral homes

Some of the ruined castles and abbeys were acquired by the newly rich and refurbished to become the family seats of those without a landed ancestry. Polesden Lacey, for example, was turned into a beautiful Edwardian house, and Lindisfarne Castle became one of the most unusual houses in Britain when it was remodelled by Sir Edwin Lutyens, who also built the medieval style Castle Drogo in Devon.

Owners of ancestral stately homes, who had not been ruined by the death duties introduced in 1894, also began to refurbish their properties. Arundel Castle was rebuilt in medieval style by the Duke of Norfolk, likewise Belvoir Castle by the Duke of Rutland. Lord Curzon rescued the keep of Tattershall Castle, and Leeds Castle in Kent was also rebuilt, becoming the most perfect evocation of a moated medieval castle in the south of England.

Conservation societies

In more recent times the romantic view that old buildings are simply 'picturesque' has been replaced by a more pragmatic one, due to the tourist phenomenon and to a more scientific approach to the question of conservation. Ancient buildings are being denuded of their clinging ivy so that their true structure can be revealed and any further deterioration caused by the plants' roots prevented.

Much of this work has been done by private

Pellwall Hall, Staffordshire, c.1898 (below). *The gardens of country houses were their owners' pride and joy just as today – when so many of them are in the care of the National Trust or similar bodies – they are a source of endless pleasure to visitors. When the houses were privately owned and had to sustain large families and their servants, the kitchen gardens were as important as the ones devoted to flowers. Here were grown all the vegetables and herbs required for the abundant Victorian diners, also apples and pears and the strawberries, raspberries, blackberries, plums and damsons that were made into home-made jams. An essential element of any garden was the greenhouse where plants could be raised and even, occasionally, a grape vine cultivated. At Pellwall Hall at least three gardeners were employed and no doubt they had many young lads to help them and to train for the next generation of gardeners.*

Spains Hall, Essex, 1902 (right). *At Spains Hall the home of the Ruggles Brise family since 1760 the lawns were kept immaculate by the gardener who used a donkey to pull the heavy lawnmower. During the 18th century the country landowners employed a vast army of servants and attendants to run thier houses. There were gardeners, in all their different forms, livery men, maids and butlers and tens of others in various jobs around the estate. The Ruggles Brise like many country house families were closely involved with the countryside in which they lived and an 18th century Thomas Ruggles became notable for his dedication to the cause of improving the condition of the agricultural labourer.*

Since 1902 when this photograph was taken the decorative creeper covering the house has been taken down and inevitably the donkey has gone too, replaced by a motorised lawn mower.

deterioration caused by the plants' roots prevented.

Much of this work has been done by private bodies and charities, supported by the subscriptions of many ordinary citizens. The most active of these organizations is the National Trust, founded by Canon Rawnsley, vicar of Crosthwaite near Keswick, and others, in 1895, who conceived the idea of forming a society to protect beautiful areas of Britain and conserve buildings of historic interest that were in danger of demolition. Today, the Trust protects some half a million acres of land and 485 miles of coastline as well as over 200 historic buildings in England and Wales. The National Trust for Scotland performs a similar function north of the Border.

Tourism has helped to ensure the preservation of the ancient buildings photographed lovingly by Francis Frith in the 19th century.

Playgrounds of the public

Where historic buildings are not preserved by public subscription, various other means have been found to ensure their survival. The development of the amusement park, for instance, demonstrates the democratic nature of modern tourism. As long ago as the 1860s it occurred to the great excursionist Thomas Cook that it would be a splendid idea if the great estates of the landed rich could be opened for visits by the common people. He wrote to Lord Shrewsbury asking permission to arrange such a visit to his lordship's estate, Alton Towers. His request was granted and soon Alton Towers became a regular outing for Victorians. Today, Alton Towers is one of the leading pleasure parks of Britain.

Thus, the lands which once gave power and influence to their owners have become the playgrounds of the general public and are thereby preserved as reminders of the long journey of the British people towards democracy. ☐

The Black Gate and Castle, Newcastle, 1901 (below). *One tends to think that history, as far as Newcastle-upon-Tyne is concerned, goes no further back than the reign of Queen Victoria. The industrialists of the age flourished in the coal-mines and shipyards of Durham and the mighty River Tyne, and much of what we know as Newcastle-upon-Tyne was not built until the 1840s or even later. But there was a past. The splendid railway bridge spanning St Nicholas Street is here seen nestling comfortably between the Norman strongholds of Black Gate and the 'new castle' keep. Tucked in beside the Gate are the workshops of Mr Beall the sculptor, whose masonry probably helped to restore it, and, as can be seen, St Nicholas Street itself is full of gleaming broughams waiting to take tired shoppers back to their homes: a picture of bustling prosperity.*

It was not to last. The industrial north-east was soon to feel the Depression, and only now is it beginning to raise its head again. Meanwhile the Black Gate and its castle still stand — only now it's the 125s that scream between them, and not the little puffers of before.

Southampton, Old Town Walls, 1891 (right). *If you look carefully, you can see an inscription written on the sloping shelf of one of the old walls' archways, or 'arcades': Bait Sold, it says, and there beside it stands the bait merchant himself. The town walls were common property then, and if one of the many hard-pressed working men of Southampton could make use of them, then he was no doubt very welcome. The bait-seller's stall is a donkey-cart, and here his only customers seem to be a group of likely lads — probably waiting to flinch a sprat or two when the bait-seller's attention is distracted by the two delightful young ladies waiting coyly in the shadows round the corner.*

Although Southampton suffered extensive bomb damage during World War II, these old arcades were spared — but no one sells bait from them any more. There is not much call for it: the fishing smacks and clipper-ships of the 1890s have grown into towering oil tankers and cruise-liners, and there are more tourists than fishermen round the old town walls today, which surprisingly have changed a great deal over the past century.

Bodiam Castle, East Surrey, 1902. *Bodiam is perhaps one of England's best-known castles. It is all a traditional castle should be, with its impressive castellations and sturdy turrets, and its moat strewn with waterlilies. It was built in the 14th century on the River Rother in East Sussex, to repel French invaders who were supposed to be sailing up from the Kent coast (they never arrived). By the time this photograph was taken, the only invaders were bonneted lady excursionists intent on soaking up the romantic atmosphere. Bodiam was particularly easy of access to Victorian visitors after 1851, when the railway station at Robertsbridge opened five miles away. A short ride in a pony and trap brought them to the portcullised drawbridge, and after crossing that they were free to explore the ivy-clad walls as they wished.*

Now the castle - stripped of its ivy - is owned by the National Trust. There are car parks and cafes and video shows to entice today's visitors but the main attraction remains the same, and it is still possible to wander in the grounds as these three ladies did, dreaming of knights and adventure.

Barnard Castle, Durham, 1890 (left). *With its solid stone-walled houses and the huge, blunt ruins from which the town takes its name, Barnard Castle looks uncompromisingly northern. It lies astride the River Tees in County Durham, amidst wild and beautiful country, and during the days of the horse and carriage it was an important travellers' stagingpost. The coachman and his passengers would 'put up' at the King's Head in the broad main street (as Dickens did in 1838, recommending its ale in his novel,* Nicholas Nickleby*) and then clatter over the sturdy, surprisingly graceful bridge towards Penrith or Durham.*

Nowadays, Barnard Castle is more geared to those visitors who want to stay and look at its treasures than those just passing through. There is a rich collection of local antiques in the Bowes Museum, some beautiful (and hardy!) landscaped gardens, viewpoints from which to contemplate the rugged grandeur of the Tees valley and, of course, the obstinate remains of the Castle itself, still keeping their centuries-old vigil over the town.

Farnham, Waverley Abbey Ruins, Surrey, 1906 (left). *That great 19th-century literary giant, Sir Walter Scott, is said to have taken the title of one of his most famous novels from the beautiful ruins of this Abbey beside the River Wey in Surrey. That fact alone was enough to make it a celebrated national monument, even though little of historical interest has survived the ravages of the Reformation. By the time this photograph was taken, some hundred years after Scott's* Waverley *was first published, the building was almost entirely overgrown, peeping out from the trees and greenery around it like one of those bizarre architectural 'follies' of which the Edwardians were so fond.*

Nowadays, Sir Walter Scott is out of fashion, and the Abbey ruin has to be seen to be appreciated by today's historians. So there Waverley stands, still crumbling, and soon all that is left of the first Cistercian Abbey in England will be forgotten.

Caernarvon Castle, Gwynedd, 1891. *Caernarvon Castle, the memorable scene of the Prince of Wales' Investiture in 1969, was perhaps best appreciated in 1891 from the sea. It also looked impressive from the landward side, with its moat and towering ramparts, but it was only from the Menai Straits that one could really appreciate its sprawling and powerful impact. To the sailors of these fishing boats the castle must have been a familiar site; ever since Edward I built it in 1282 there had been working vessels of one kind or another moored up beside its three great seaward walls. In the meantime, the buildings within had crumbled away and all that was left was this mighty shell and some overgrown rubble — nothing at all for tourists.*

Now the emphasis has changed. The whole castle was given a huge spring clean for the television cameras in 1969 and since then, most of its visitors have been able to explore the sparkling stonework from the well-kept lawns within its walls. The boats moored in the water, however, have not gone, merely changed to plastic and fibreglass.

Leeds Castle, Kent, 1892. *Leeds Castle has always had an air of exclusivity about it. It was built between the 9th and 14th centuries on three islands in a picturesque lake deep in the Kent countryside, and was known as 'The Queens' Castle', until the reign of Henry V. There the highest ladies of the land lived with their kings and courtiers ensconced in medieval splendour. When this photograph was taken in 1892, the castle was kept strictly private, and could only be glimpsed by wayfarers along what is now the A20 through the trees of the surrounding parkland. This sense of mystery, combined with the legends of its royal past and its fairy-tale appearance, no doubt evoked the Poet Laureate Lord Tennyson's fashionable ballads of high-born English chivalry and romance. Today, the castle is much the same except, suprisingly, the chimneys have been removed.*

Windsor Castle, Berkshire, 1895 (above). *Ever since it was first founded by William the Conqueror, Windsor Castle has belonged to Britain's royal family. There could be no more idealistic view than this, showing the vast round tower with its Union Jack fluttering in the breeze, St George's Chapel to the right, the delicate grandeur of Eton College Chapel over the bridge and in the foreground, swans drifting by and the flower of England's youth out boating on the Thames. It was enough to make the Imperial heart swell: the Queen's in her Castle, all's right with the world.*

Now Windsor is no longer a stronghold of all that is most British — only a symbol of it. The town is full of American and Japanese tourists, queuing up to troop around the Castle, and the stretch of river below Eton is choked with blaring pleasure cruisers. But on a summer's morning when the flag still flies and the chapel music floats across the water, it is still just possible to recall the supreme confidence and patriotic fervour felt by the Victorians of 1895.

Haddon Hall, Derbyshire, 1886 (right). *This wonderfully positioned castle represented the essence of romance to the fin-de-siècle imagination: it was set in resplendent countryside, and bathed in delicious mystery. The Hall was built successively between the 14th and 17th centuries, close to the Derbyshire town of Bakewell and overlooking the upper reaches of the River Wye. Its early owners, the Vernons married into the family of the Dukes of Rutland; when they moved to Belvoir Castle in 1700, the magnificent Hall fell empty, and mysteriously stayed so for a full two hundred years.*

Paradoxically, it is thanks to this long period of dereliction that Haddon Hall still stands as such a sturdy example of pre-18th-century grandeur today. When the Duke of Rutland began to restore it as a family home in 1900, the 'improving' whims of Georgian and mid-Victorian architects with all their mock-Gothic excesses had mercifully just gone out of fashion. And so the Hall we can visit today is essentially just the same as it was not only when this photograph was taken, but two hundred years before then.

Alton Towers, Staffordshire, 1898 (below). *The 15th Earl of Shrewsbury created Alton Towers and its gardens out of a wild landscape just before Queen Victoria came to the throne. Six hundred acres of barren hillside were planted with the exotic shrubs and trees that had been introduced into England in the 18th century by botanists such as Sir Joseph Banks. A vast neo-gothic mansion was built in the midst of the estate and greenhouses and pergolas were erected along the walks, and this splendid and beautiful park became a famous 19th century beauty spot.*

The gardens, Alton Towers, 1898 (right). *The glorious gardens of Alton Towers combined the natural look created by Capability Brown and the formal design of Italian gardens with urns and statues to add interest to the walks. As early as the 1850s Thomas Cook obtained permission from Lord Shrewsbury to take his Temperance customers to Alton Towers but was reprimanded because some of them got drunk and behaved badly. What Lord Shrewsbury would say of today's Alton Towers with its giant racers, corkscrew rides and other fairground attractions is difficult to imagine.*

Stonehenge, Wiltshire, 1887 (below). *The mysterious stone circles of Salisbury Plain have never been satisfactorily explained and continue to inspire wonder and amazement, even in our sceptical age. In 1887 it was still possible to walk among the giant monoliths, but this is now prohibited for fear of the damage done by a few of the thousands of visitors who come every year. Some of the giant stones were transported to Salisbury Plain from as far away as South Wales — one has recently been discovered at the bottom of the Bristol Channel; others came from the nearer Marlborough Downs. There is no doubt that the circles were a kind of temple and served a religion based on sun worship. Around the central stones is a circle of holes, now filled with concrete, in which other stones may have rested.*

The Roman Baths, Bath, 1890 (right). *The mineral waters of Bath led to the development of this exceptionally lovely Georgian town in the 18th century. Under the direction of Beau Nash, the spa became the most fashionable in Britain. But it is the Roman Baths which are the focal point of the ancient historical roots of the city.*

The Roman baths were not discovered until the 19th century, a little before this photograph was taken. The waters that fed the Pump Room and other parts of the Spa had also supplied water for the Roman baths, the largest of which was lead-lined and sumptuously decorated. More relics of the Roman town have since been unearthed and are now exhibited in the museum which is among the many attractions that have made Bath one of the most visited cities in Britain.

Mansions of Learning

Education has always been more a matter of expediency than human welfare. In medieval times the sons of Barons and Knights acquired their knowledge of the arts of war at the courts of friends, and others learned how to administrate large estates as students at monastries. The growth of trade and commerce increased the demand for education and by the 18th century there were schools for the sons of merchants. With the Industrial Revolution there began a need to increase the mental capabilities of workers, and Britain moved gradually into the era of education for all.

Kings College, Cambridge, 1890. *Tradition has it that Cambridge University was founded by a group of desperate scholars who fled to the fens in the 13th century after a particularly bloody dispute with the sorely-tried citizens of Oxford. Whichever came first, Oxford and Cambridge are undisputedly the oldest universities in Britain, and their cities boast some of the country's finest academic buildings. King's College is the most sublime of all. Built by Henry VI, it was established as a sister college to Eton and until 1870 — just 20 years before the date of this photograph — its undergraduates were exclusively old-Etonians, exempt by this privilege alone from university examinations. Its pinnacled and honey-coloured chapel sits on the 'backs' of the River Cam and has come to represent the essence of the 'Oxbridge' ethos.*

King's College is perhaps best-known nowadays as the venue of the annual Festival of Nine Lessons and Carols: a Christmas institution as beautiful and evocative as the College itself.

Travellers in Britain often come across small, red-brick buildings with slate roofs, topped occasionally with a small bell tower. Their style is faintly Gothic, one or two windows with pointed arches, for instance, and belltowers on the roofs. Built as schools in the 19th century, there is a faintly religious air about them, even when they have been converted into museums or private houses. This is perhaps not so surprising for learning and religion have been closely associated since the Middle Ages when the church was the repository of the knowledge that had almost been lost in many parts of Europe during the Dark Ages.

The small brick schools of the 19th century were not, however, church schools but represented the first national attempt to bring secular education to everyone. As such, these modest buildings have their place in history alongside grander establishments built to encourage the pursuit of knowledge, to provide the nation with people able to guide its destiny, to man its industries and houses of commerce, and to preserve its culture. They are as much architectural landmarks of educational progress as the centuries-old grammar schools, the more renowned public schools and the superb colleges of the ancient universities of both Oxford and Cambridge.

Attitudes towards education

In the mid-19th century, despite the fact that the Industrial Revolution was making demands on the brain as well as on the sinews of the young, education was at a low ebb. Agricultural workers, who still numbered half the population, had never thought that education was a necessity, and the urban poor could not afford it. Indeed, it never occurred to them to send their children to school.

Even many of the rich and aristocratic chose to send their sons to school partly to be rid of them during adolescence; a few employed private tutors

Old Grammar School, Market Harborough, 1922 (left, above). *As the town's name implies, markets have long been held there, dating back at least to 1203. The town still has a twice-weekly general market.*

So strong was the market tradition that when Robert Smyth founded and built the Old Grammar School in the centre of town in 1614, he raised it on wooden pillars, thus making room for the butter market, which was held there for generations.

The Old Grammar School, photographed here in 1922 with the porch of the 13th-century Church of St Dionysius in the background, is no longer a grammar school. It is now used for meetings and receptions.

The High School, Bedford, 1897 (left, below). *The county town of Bedfordshire, Bedford has also been an educational centre since the 16th century, when a Bedford-born Lord Mayor of London, Sir William Harpur, left land in trust, the income from which was to be used to finance the Harpur Trust schools.*

Today, Bedford has as many as four public schools, including Bedford Modern School, founded in 1566, and Bedford High School, a girls' public school, shown here in a photograph taken in 1897. Sometime earlier the great theological writer John Bunyan exerted a considerable influence on English thought and was jailed in Bedford for 12 years for his ideas.

Harlaxton School, Lincolnshire, 1890 (below). *The village school at Harlaxton, three miles south-west of Grantham, has been called a 'Disneyesque fantasia'. It is a prominent building in a village largely rebuilt in the first half of the 19th century as a setting for the vast Harlaxton Hall, built by George de Ligne-Gregory, owner of the Harlaxton estate, between 1822 and 1837.*

The school, to the right of the Church of St Mary and St Peter in this photograph, is a half-timbered, brick building with ashlar dressing and terracotta ornaments. The church was the victim of much enthusiastic rebuilding and excessive restoration work during the 19th century, but traces of Norman and Gothic can still be detected.

Eton, Berkshire, 1909 (above). *Since Henry VI founded Eton as the King's College of Our Lady of Eton in 1440, it has been favoured by kings and aristocrats. George III's great affection for the College is reciprocated by the annual celebration of his birthday on 4 June when old boys, their parents and visitors assemble for picnic lunches and the Procession of Boats.*

Royal patronage seemed to help Eton through the Reformation, despite Henry VIII trying to take some of its revenue. Though founded as a free school, Eton began to take paying pupils, and at the beginning of the 19th century the provost was summoned by a select committee to defend the school against complaints by scholars that they were being robbed while the college grew rich. In 1883, Henry VI's statutes were revoked and the stipulation that Foundation scholars had to be poor was withdrawn. Today, few can enter unless rich or well connected.

Harrow on the Hill, Middlesex, 1914 (right). *Harrow School began its life as a free school established by John Lyon in the Elizabethan Age, but by the 19th century had become an expensive fee-paying school. The strict conditions of school routine laid down by the founder had been forgotten. School revolts were not infrequent in the 19th century; in one of them Richard Wellesley, brother of the later Duke of Wellington, was one of the ring leaders.*

In the photograph above, right, the boys, wearing the traditional Harrow boater, introduced in the 19th century, are waiting for Bill or roll call. The 19th century was a period of recovery and consolidation for Harrow, which became much sought-after as a school for the sons of the affluent middleclasses, and many of its traditions began then, among them Harrow football and the traditional school songs. Today, the school has changed little from Victorian Times though the boys who attend are more cosmopolitan.

to educate their sons at home. A boy's education might be completed by his tutor taking him on a version of the 18th-century gentleman's Grand Tour, which, according to contemporary reports, was often more of a protracted orgy than an educational experience.

Inadequacy of schools

Ironically, when the demand for an educated class was increasing, the educational system, such as it was, had sunk into a state of ramshackle neglect and needed serious attention. It had never catered for the whole population, for academic learning had been essential only to the administrators and scholars of society, not to the bulk of the people. The change during the 19th century from rural to town life with its multiplicity of new industrial activities and their clerical superstructure during the 19th century demanded people with at least an elementary knowledge of reading, writing and arithmetic.

The educational establishments inherited by the early Victorians were for the most part of ancient origin. Many of them were in imposing buildings which in themselves were landmarks of British history but their fine architecture tended to disguise the often inadequate curriculum offered.

Influence of the church

The earliest attempts at education in Britain were fostered by the church which once played an important part in the administration of rural life in Britain. Every abbey and monastery had a school in which boys from the local community were taught Latin which was not only the language of the church but also the common language of Europe. These early schools would often have less than 100 pupils. There were about 550 such schools in England and Wales during the reigns of the Plantagenet kings but they had an effect far beyond their numbers in medieval Europe, exerting a civilizing influence in rough and turbulent times similar to Alcuin of York, for example, who was invited by Charlemagne to found schools in his Holy Roman Empire.. These schools taught Latin grammar (hence the term 'grammar' schools) and other classical subjects. St Peter's in York and Winchester (the oldest public school in England, founded in 1382) both still exist.

Tudor times

When Henry VIII dissolved the monasteries in the 16th century, many monastic schools such as those at Canterbury, Ely and Rochester were reconstituted, being given royal charters and often taking the name of 'King's School'.

There was little incentive for the population as a whole to become educated, though new schools were established in order to provide the nation with educated administrators. Edward VI, continuing Henry VIII's role as a promoter of schooling for the people, founded such schools as Christ's Hospital, where Coleridge, Lamb and Leigh Hunt were later educated, and in Elizabeth I's reign Harrow and Rugby were started. Eton had already been founded by Henry VI in 1440 as the King's College of Our Lady of Eton.

Rivalry of religious groups

In the following centuries education tended to stagnate, with little effort being made for anyone other than those directly involved with the royal court or the landed families. Most of the population remained illiterate and ignorant, with no attempt being made to educate them until the 19th century. Education for the people became a crusade for religious organizations at a time when religion permeated every aspect of national life and conditioned people's behaviour as much as a desire for material achievement does today.

Monmouth, Gwent, 1896 (above). *Although its buildings were only 30 years old when this photograph was taken (the original ones having been demolished), Monmouth Grammar School was, in fact, founded in the early 17th century. William Jones, who endowed it, was a successful Merchant of the City of London who remembered his home town over the border in Wales and set up an institution for its brightest boys where they might learn, as his motto has it, to 'Serve and Obey'. In 1896, the principle on which the grammar school was established was much the same: Monmouth's privileged children studied there, either through the good offices of the endowment fund or by paying fees.*

The school is one of the comparatively few independent grammar schools left in Britain. Added to the Victorian buildings shown here are modern squash courts and such like — a far cry from the meagre facilities of William Jones' day when 'grammar' meant Latin and little else.

Winchester, Hampshire, 1896 (right). *The handsome Hampshire city of Winchester has long revolved around its two most important institutions: the Cathedral and the College. William of Wykeham, who founded and established Winchester College and its sister establishment of New College at Oxford, was Bishop of Winchester from 1367-1404. The school soon became one of the country's most fashionable: a fitting place of learning for gentlemen's sons and a useful entrance into academe. The joint motto of both Winchester and New College said it all: 'Manners Makyth Man'.*

The city's prosperity, so obvious from Frith's marvellously detailed photograph, still depends to a large extent on the College. The sons of gentlemen are not the only scholars now, however, and although Winchester is still a fashionable public school, it has an enviable academic reputation to maintain. As at Oxford, today's scholars must earn their keep intellectually, or not at all.

Educational activity was divided and, indeed, became a cause of rivalry among many religious groups, including the established Church of England, the Dissenters, Baptists, Congregationalists and Wesleyan Methodists and Roman Catholics. The latter had been allowed to evacuate their schools from France during the French Revolution and had set up Downside, Ampleforth, Stoneyhurst and other Catholic schools in England.

Lack of discipline

Consequently, there was a church presence in every aspect of 19th-century education; not only were there church schools but every school, including those that had been endowed by rich, secular merchants as far back as the 16th century, had a strong cast of ordained ministers among the teaching staff and a dedication to a classical curriculum in which Latin and Greek loomed large. This was particularly true of public schools where, like the grammar schools, the standards of teaching and discipline had deteriorated to such an extent that students frequently revolted, threw away their books and indulged in often riotous and licentious behaviour.

Similar tendencies were evident in the ancient universities of Oxford and Cambridge; according to the report of a Royal Commission on Oxford in 1832 the students mostly dedicated themselves to sensual vices which, as W.J. Reader remarks in his *Life in Victorian Times*, was 'a revealing comment on an institution in which students were mostly intending to take Holy Orders'.

Elementary education

For the aspiring middle-class parent wishing to give his son (education for a woman was not considered necessary) a good start in life, the educational prospects at the beginning of Victoria's reign were not encouraging.

Wells, Somerset, 1890 (below). *The cathedral city of Wells looks today almost as it did nearly a century ago. The market place, pictured here, was its temporal centre and the cathedral, whose four-square tower rears up in the background, its spiritual heart. Wells cathedral has always dominated this picturesque Somerset city — in more ways than one. When this photograph was taken, there would have been far more bustle in the Cathedral Close behind the turreted Gate than here in the market place: there, the religious population of the city would be going about its ecclesiastical business between the Bishop's Palace, his church and the Cathedral School. All three institutions brought prosperity to Wells; the Bishop's diocese (including nearby Bath) was a particularly rich one and the school — still going strong — has been a prestigious centre of musical excellence ever since its medieval beginnings.*

Bath, Avon, 1890 (right). *Education is not only a matter of schools and universities but also an understanding of the manners and mores of the society in which one lives. In the 18th and 19th centuries much of this kind of social education was found in places like Bath. No self-respecting student of society would dare forego a season there, with regular visits to the Pump Room, a night or two at the Theatre and a stroll along Pulteney Bridge across the Weir. Bath was the place to see and be seen: one 'paraded up and down for an hour,' wrote Miss Austen, 'looking at everybody and speaking to no-one.' Even in 1890, when this view was taken, visitors were more likely to study their fellow tourists than the glorious Georgian architecture with which the city abounds.*

Although Bath is no longer de rigueur *as far as the British social calendar is concerned, it draws many more tourists today than ever before.*

Uppingham, Leicestershire, 1927 (left). *Uppingham School was founded in 1584 as a grammar school, and so it remained, a fairly mediocre establishment for local Leicestershire boys, until the middle of the 19th century. Then, in 1853, Edward Thring arrived as head-master and during the next 30 years Uppingham was transformed into one of England's leading public schools. Thring was a disciple of Thomas Arnold, the celebrated headmaster of Rugby who more or less invented the public school system. Both men believed their institutions should be disciplined training grounds where Britain's 'Christian gentlemen' might learn how to behave in future professional life, and their schools were hierarchial microcosms of the country they helped to mould.*

Today's public schools are a little different from how they used to be. Uppingham admits girls now – unheard of even in the 1920s when this rather dour photograph of the High Street was taken.

Cathedral School, Hereford, 1891 (above). *Like Lincoln, the attractive city of Hereford sits in what was once a quiet corner of England, nurtured by the land around it (here rich in fruit and hops) and presided over by its kindly and noble cathedral. It was perfectly self-sufficient, and grew through the ages into a prodigious seat of learning. Its cathedral school received its status in 1583, though there is evidence of a school existing in 1385 when the Bishop complained of the lack of a fit master. Evidence of Hereford's educational role lies in the astonishingly rich collection of books in the cathedral's ancient chained library.*

By 1891 Hereford had become an important staging-post between Wales and the Midlands. Here, railway, road and river met, visitors began exploring the other streets and soon the quiet Cathedral Close became a favourite 'sight' for tourists on the way to or from the romantic Black Mountains and Beacons.

For the poor and destitute it was almost hopeless – though not entirely so, for there were some people looking at the miserable lot of many in the overcrowded cities, who felt a desire to correct the ills of society. It was obvious to them that the educated would have a better chance in life than the illiterate and ignorant, and numerous organizations therefore grew up to instruct the poor, among them the London City Missions and the Ragged Schools Society. The latter was run by volunteers and offered elementary reading and writing lessons to children, most of whom attended barefoot and in ragged clothes.

Though a mere drop in the sea of illiteracy, these efforts had brought some 15,000 children to the threshold of education by 1870, the year that the Elementary Education Act was passed by Parliament, some of whose members had in the past been reluctant to provide education for the poor on the grounds that it would only lead them to have ideas above their station.

The 1870 Act was the first step towards the universal education that has become the right of every child in Britain today. The Act also prompted the building of numerous schools, modest in scale, but many of which are still used today.

Dilemma of Victorian middle classes

The rising middle classes of Victorian Britain, faced with the deterioration of the existing grammar and public schools, found themselves on the horns of a dilemma. Public schools, whatever their inadequacies, were attended by the sons of the ruling classes and were thus valuable for making useful contacts, but because of their inherited commitment to the classics they hardly provided the education that a member of the new industrial world required for his offspring.

The answer to this dilemma lay in following the advice of Samuel Smiles who believed that the

Oxford University

Oxford University is reputed to have been established in 1167 with the migration of scholars from Paris. It was towards the end of the 13th century that Oxford developed the collegiate system, the paradigm for all subsequent British Universities. This collection of independent colleges and halls, was monastic in origin and each had its own rules and regulations. As religious influences began to wane during the 17th century and the university became more centralized, special buildings were commissioned for the colleges to share.

The Clarendon Building, 1890 (below). *The Clarendon Building, standing in slightly faded Palladian splendour in the centre of the picture, housed the Oxford University Press, and the Sheldonian Theatre next door was designed by Sir Christopher Wren to accommodate all the University's major ceremonies, including the ritual 'matriculation', of each student at the beginning of his university career, and the conferment of his degree at the end.*

With the neat shopfront of Blackwell's The Bookseller across the street, Broad Street became dedicated to the pursuit of knowledge. Pursuing knowledge, however, was not the average student's favourite pastime in 1890 — which may account for the deserted nature of the street in the photograph. Now, of course, Broad Street is never quiet!

Eights Week, 1906 (left). 'Eights Week' was, at the time of this photograph, the highlight of the summer (or 'Trinity') term at Oxford. Everything stopped for 'Eights', and as soon as the right time came around late each May, the entire university would repair to the Cherwell to watch the college rowing teams – 'eights' – compete against one another for the coveted title of 'Head of the River'. For the few who took part in the water, it was a chance to show off their brawn (so often in greater supply than brain amongst the more affluent colleges) to the many who crowded around the boathouses and barges to watch. It was an elaborate social occasion. One wore boater and blazer, sipped punch and champagne, and spoke of the 'Commem Balls' to come.

Little has changed. 'Eights Week' is still the university's favourite summer celebration. Now there are women's teams, of course (a terrible innovation to traditionalists), and perhaps the champagne is a little less free-flowing, but the boaters and blazers and festival atmosphere are just the same. They are all part of the tradition that helps to hold Oxford together.

Old Oxford, Cornmarket, 1922 (right). One of the earliest statutes of the medieval University of Oxford – and one that still stands today – ruled that no student should live more than six miles away from Carfax. Carfax was the name of the crossroads at the southern end of Cornmarket and managed to survive, like St Michael's Tower on the right, as one of the few reminders of Oxford's pre-university past. Cornmarket was old Oxford's principal thoroughfare; its name is self-explanatory and, although it had long lost its original occupation by the time of this photograph, it always strongly resisted the encroachment of nearby university buildings. This was where the college servants and students did their shopping: one of the few places where town met gown in mutual satisfaction.

Cornmarket is still a shopping street: so much so that a huge chromium-plated 'precinct' has erupted in the middle of it and cars, for which there is no longer any room, have been banned. It is the busiest and now, sadly, the most modern-looking street in ancient central Oxford.

future was in the hands of those capable of helping themselves. While many parents opted for either a grammar or public school for their sons, others combined to create new schools which would have a curriculum suitable to the needs of the people on whose shoulders the Industrial Revolution was being supported.

The creation of numerous proprietary schools, mechanics' institutes and other such bodies exerted an influence on the grammar and public schools themselves and stimulated a great revival in standards of education for the 18 million people in need of it, according to the statistics published in Schools for the People in 1871 by G.C.T. Bartley, who added that of this number only 1,384,203 were receiving an education of some kind or another, however inadiquate.

Progress of universal education

Since those days the progress of universal education may have faltered at times but has always moved forward, achieving education for women, the entry to university by merit and not through influence and money, the creation of technological colleges, and the raising of the school-leaving age to 16. The dream of free and equal education for all has been achieved. In the evolution of our educational system it has added to the landscape and to our national heritage superb monastic buildings, elegant Tudor and Jacobean public school mansions, Georgian grammar schools, Victorian educational and technical institutions and humble brick schoolrooms that tell the story of a great human and national achievement.

Progress in education is, however, a continuing movement, and the twentieth century has bought great and taxing new challenges to the existing educational systems which now have to adapt to a more international world, and a rich and varied multi-racial society. ☐

Oxford, view on the Cherwell, 1906 (above). *There are two rivers in Oxford. One is the Isis (or Thames) which laps leisurely along the western boundaries of the university, and the other is the more picturesque Cherwell. The stretch of the Cherwell between Christ Church Meadows and the University Parks is especially pleasant: just the place for the Edwardian beau to take his chaperoned lady-friend out punting. Inevitably, there were strict rules to be obeyed in the matter of punting. First, one was obliged to wear the right clothes. For the punter, these should be 'whites', preferably with college boater and tie and for the punted, a cream, satin-sashed gown and shady parasol. Often punt-parties would take their own supply of Chablis or Champagne, trailed in the waters of the river to keep it cool, and sometimes a fashionable horned gramophone was hauled aboard too. This was how the university enjoyed itself.*

It still does. Women are allowed to do the punting now (they can even wear jeans if they like) and the well-bred strains of the gramophone would be drowned today in reggae tapes, but 80 years on, the view on the Cherwell on any summer afternoon is surprisingly the same.

Lincoln, 1890. *Pushed to the edge of England, well away from the main thorough-fares from north to south, and all but submerged in the waters of The Wash and the North Sea, Lincolnshire is one of the least-known of our counties. It is like an island within an island, with Lincoln as its capital. Here a Norman Bishop chose a rare hill on which to build his Cathedral and its school and, at its foot, a bustling and self-contained city soon grew up. By the time this photograph was taken, Lincoln was living well off the fat of the land: its principal twin industries then, as now, were agriculture and horticulture.*

The county town's affluence can be seen in its crowded cobbled street; flags flying and awnings out against the Fenland sun, it is a picture of confident well-being.

Lincoln is just as proud a place today as it was in 1890. The wide fields and acres of bulbs that surround the town are even more prodigious now than they used to be (thanks to the huge machines and glasshouses that sprawl over the fertile soil) and the streets of the city itself are crowded with the tourists who have found their way at last to one of Britain's best-kept secrets.

Beverley, Humberside, c.1880. *In what used to be called the East Riding of Yorkshire and is now less romantically known as Humberside, the pleasant market town of Beverley sits comfortably between the Wolds and the estuary at Hull. Its most splendid days were already over when the photographer arrived: the tomb of the monastic settlement's founder was no longer a favourite place of pilgrimage (between the 10th and 15th centuries it was thought that a visit to St John of Beverley all but guaranteed victory in battle), and the road from Hull to York was not as busy as it had been in the port's heyday. But if the stately and extravagant Minster reveals Beverley's past importance, the wide, neatly cobbled streets and well-turned-out children in the foreground of this photograph suggest that it was still quite an affluent town in Victorian times.*

The founder of Beverley Grammar School, which was situated in the Cathedral precincts, was St John of Beverley who had been a student at King's School, Canterbury, a master at St Peter's, York and came to Beverley Grammar School in the 12th century. A school already existed in 704 but it was St John of Beverley who gave it renown.

Durham, 1892. So far away from the civilized south and so close to the inhospitable border of Scotland, Durham was for many centuries regarded as an outpost of the kingdom. If that were so, it could only have been in a geographical sense, for it has been rich in culture and learning since its foundation as a city in the 11th century.

The Cathedral Grammar School was probably founded in the 10th century after the removal of St Cuthbert's monastery from Lindisfarne to Durham in 995. Originally the school was in Palace Green but moved to its present site above the River Wear in 1844.

The Cathedral of Christ and the Blessed Virgin, pictured here in all its stern magnificence, was erected on a rocky promontory almost encircled by the River Wear: here the followers of St Cuthbert, who built it, could study and pray in peace and safety.

One of the country's foremost early scholars, the Venerable Bede (673-735) was buried in Durham Cathedral — and a tradition of scholarship has blossomed in the sharp northern air ever since. Durham University (inset one of the new colleges) was founded on the same collegiate pattern as Oxford and Cambridge and is still one of Britain's most successful.

Norwich, 1919. *For several centuries after the Norman Bishop Herbert de Losinga built his Cathedral at Norwich, the city was divided. The ecclesiastical population, who lived and studied around the Cathedral Close, set themselves apart from (and probably above) the uneducated townspeople and each kept very much to his own. By 1919, relations between church and laity were somewhat more comfortable and Norwich had settled into the relaxed city pictured here by Frith. Bishop Bridge, spanning the River Wensum to the south-east of the city, is just a few hundred yards from the Bishop's House and his Cathedral — but apart from the graceful spire in the background, there is little to suggest it. The Wensum looks more like a canal here, with a handy waterside inn and a well-laden boat moored up by the bridge.*

Now there is less traffic on the river, and much more over it than in 1919, but the streets beyond Bishop Bridge are essentially the same.

Exeter, 1896. *The county town of Devon is particularly proud of its Guildhall. It was built in the 15th century and is now one of the oldest municipal buildings still standing in England. In the photograph it is shown wedged between the shops and stores of the busy High Street, in its element as an ancient centre of commerce and craft. A Guild was an association set up by the merchants of a given city for their own protection as traders – a sort of forerunner of the trades unions. Their hall was a natural advertisement of their prosperity and so the finer it looked, the better. The merchants of the city, discontented with their high school, insisted on the foundation of a free school and won their case against the Dean and chapter who had maintained that no new schools would be established within seven miles of the city.*

Like Coventry, Exeter suffered severe damage in the bombing raids of World War II, but happily the Guildhall (with the glorious Cathedral and its Close) survived intact. Although still used for civic functions, the mere public are now allowed to admire the Guild coats-of-arms, portraits and previous regalia kept in Guildhall. The dignified splendour of the exterior of the building looks even more incongruous surrounded by the modern shops than it did in 1896.

Cambridge University

In 1209, following 'disturbances' in Oxford between scholars and towns-folk, a number of academics left for Cambridge where they set up their own 'universitas' (from the French meaning guild or corporation). Soon the University grew and the collegiate system developed with the founding of Peterhouse in 1284.

Today Cambridge is very much a cosmopolitan sort of place with its grand colleges, age old customs, heady mix of academia and student high jinks. Tourists from all over the world come to punt on Scudamores' boats past Kings and under the mathematician's Bridge, or up to Granchester where they may take a drink at the riverside pub or ask 'is there honey still for tea?'.

Fitzwilliam Museum, 1890 (below). *The Fitzwilliam Museum was one of the earliest public museums ever to be opened in Britain, as befits such a venerable city as Cambridge. The impressive neo-classical building seen here fronting Trumpington Street was commissioned in 1837 to house the collection of art and antiquities bequeathed to the city and its University in 1816 by Viscount Fitzwilliam. It was to be a showcase of civilization's finest work, designed in true 19th-century style both to instruct and to inspire.*

The Museum flourished during the Victorian era. In a country at the zenith of its own Imperial prowess — and in a city itself full of budding Empire-builders — anything that could reflect the glory of former golden ages was particularly popular. As its reputation grew, it attracted new bequests and more and more visitors. Now, the 'Fitzwilly', as it is affectionately known, has the double distinction of being not only one of the first but one of the foremost of Britain's treasure houses.

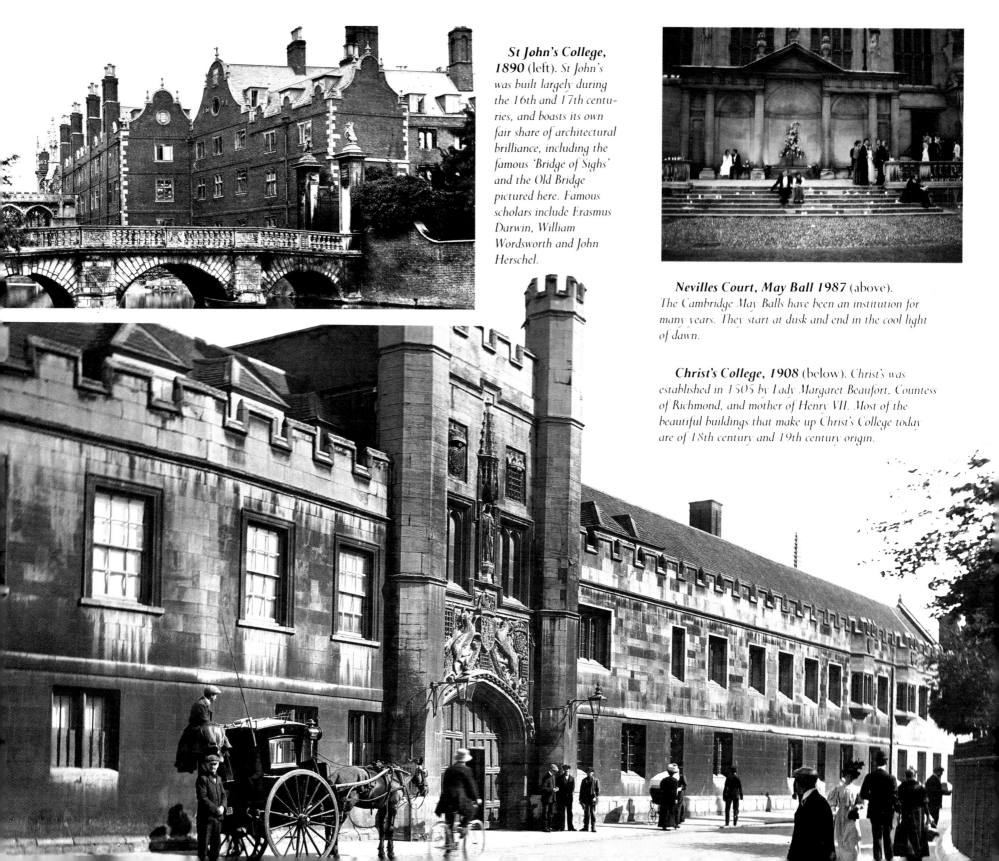

St John's College, 1890 (left). *St John's was built largely during the 16th and 17th centuries, and boasts its own fair share of architectural brilliance, including the famous 'Bridge of Sighs' and the Old Bridge pictured here. Famous scholars include Erasmus Darwin, William Wordsworth and John Herschel.*

Nevilles Court, May Ball 1987 (above). *The Cambridge May Balls have been an institution for many years. They start at dusk and end in the cool light of dawn.*

Christ's College, 1908 (below). *Christ's was established in 1505 by Lady Margaret Beaufort, Countess of Richmond, and mother of Henry VII. Most of the beautiful buildings that make up Christ's College today are of 18th century and 19th century origin.*

Salisbury, Wiltshire, 1887 (left). *The finest church building in England, the jewel in the country's crown since it was built in the 13th century, Salisbury Cathedral has become a symbol of Britain's religious and cultural heritage. Its delicately latticed spire — at 404 feet (130m) the highest in England and visible for miles from the surrounding Wiltshire countryside — soars above the ordered streets and well-kept meadows of the ancient city, and the velvety lawns and gardens of its Close exude an atmosphere of peaceful security.*

Melrose Abbey, 1890 (above). *The abbey of Melrose which was founded by David I of Scotland in 1136, was badly damaged during the wars with the English. What remains is, however, a treasured relic of the British heritage. Its preservation was due in large part to the efforts of Sir Walter Scott who, with the Duke of Buccleuch, campaigned to have it recognised as a building of historic and cultural interest.*

Melrose Abbey is visited today by thousands during the summer months, but the crowds have not spoiled the impressive isolation of this historic building.

Making a Living

The agricultural community that was England passed away in the 19th century as the population was obliged to move to industrial and mining areas to make a living. The change from country to urban life and from manual to machine labour, caused a decay in craftsmanship and individual enterprise, a process that has continued into the 20th century when crafts have almost become extinct and small traders and shopkeepers are fast disappearing.

Iron and steel works, Scunthorpe, Humberside, 1904. When the photograph (opposite) of the Frodingham Iron and Steel works at Scunthorpe was taken, the demand for its production was at its height. The construction of 'Number 4' furnace was underway and was, when commissioned, the first mechanically charged blast furnace in Europe. It was known as 'The Yankie' from the American company 'McKee' whose design it followed. Since then iron and steel consumption has declined throughout the world and numerous plants have closed down including this one. On the site are the new British Steel Administration Buildings shown left. Like many of the places which attained fame and fortune during the 19th century as a result of the Industrial Revolution, Scunthorpe was a small cluster of villages just over a hundred years ago.

The story of Scunthorpe is told at the Borough Museum and a reminder of its even earlier history remains in the 12th century church at Frodingham.

At the beginning of the 19th century the population of Britain was about 11 million; by 1837 when Victoria came to the throne it had doubled and by the end of the century it had reached nearly 40 million, most of whom lived and worked in towns and cities. The number of farm workers decreased from over 1.3 million in the mid-century to half that number by 1890. This trend was also apparent in the decline in the numbers of craftsmen, carriers, shopkeepers and others who supplied services to country people.

Work in the country had always been hard and the rewards meagre but in the 19th century, with the industrialization of Britain and the doctrines of Free Trade in the ascendant, working conditions worsened. Small farmers scarcely managed on their few acres and their standard of living was often barely above that of their labourers, who were paid less than ten shillings (50p) a week. Larger farms, which increased in number as small farmers were driven to sell up, were able to survive, the increased demand from the industrial towns producing a measure of affluence until imported grain and foodstuffs from America flooded the market.

There were some compensations for the country worker, although even these gradually vanished as economic pressures obliged labourers to sell the vegetables and fruit they grew in their cottage gardens, and even the pig which they kept to slaughter for the salted pork and smoked bacon that would provide their meat for the year.

Domestic service

It is hardly surprising that most country parents, crammed into their one- or two-roomed cottages with five or more children, were eager to see them grow up and go out to work as soon as they were ten years old. Domestic service was one of the main forms of employment for those country girls who were not needed to help on the land. Towards

Lacemaking, Devon, 1880s (left). *Lacemaking was a widespread cottage industry in Victorian times and old ladies sitting outside their houses with a pillow on their knees was a common sight in summer. The bobbins, radiating from the centre of the work, held the threads and the small cushion the pins that would mark the design as the old lady's deft hands flipped the bobbins one way or another to build up the lace pattern. The finished article earned very little money for the maker but was expensive by the time it reached the shops and was used to decorate a dress for a fashionable lady.*

During the 19th century lace became a factory product in which certain industrial cities such as Leicester and Nottingham specialized. Today, most manufactured lace comes from places like Hong Kong, Taiwan and Korea where labour is cheaper than in Europe.

The village smithy, Alderley, Gloucestershire, 1896 (below). *The village blacksmith was a busy man in 1896 for the horse was still the main form of transport in the country. There were shire horses to pull heavy weights, horses for the gigs and carts, hunters, ponies and race horses. Relieved of being both a blacksmith and a veterinary surgeon by the formation of the Royal College of Veterinary Surgeons, the farrier could concentrate on the job of shoeing horses. This was itself a highly skilled job for the farrier had to know the horse's anatomy and the ills that its hooves and legs were prone to. The shoes were made by the farrier who would recommend those appropriate to the horse's work. The farrier would also fit the shoe, first preparing the hoof and then nailing it correctly. Finally, the hoof would be rasped to ensure a neat finish.*

the latter part of the 19th century it was estimated that nearly a third of the female population of Britain were servants, in the large houses of the remaining squirearchy, in those of the rising industrial magnates or as the sole servant of some family of the rising middle class and even of those hovering between middle and working class, for servant girls were cheap to hire.

Work in a large country or town house was perhaps the most agreeable occupation, for servants had their own community and their own part of the house, and they were generally well-fed, housed and given a uniform. In the big house they were ruled over by the butler or the housekeeper and each had his or her own allotted function as kitchen maid, scullery maid, children's nursemaid or the countless other tasks which were necessary to the running of a large mansion. Girls in such service were paid between £30 and £50 a year and, as their bed/board was provided, were able to save a little towards the day when, they hoped, marriage would give them their freedom. Girls who served the less affluent and more demanding sections of society were less fortunate. Often relegated to some damp basement or draughty attic, they lived solitary lives constantly being ordered about by often despotic women and, if they were pretty, frequently at the mercy of lecherous males of the household.

Employment prospects

By the end of the century, prospects for girls were changing. Country-bred Laura, heroine of Flora Thompson's *Lark Rise to Candleford*, was 14 when she began her working life in the early 1890s as an assistant in a small town Post Office. The postal services had in fact been providing respectable work for girls for some time. And in the wings, as it were, was the typewriter, the first commercially successful version of which had been marketed in

Fisherwives, Tenby, Dyfed, 1890 (above). *These Tenby fishwives make a rugged-looking quartet, their faces revealing the hard life of the fishing folk of their day. Before the internal combustion engine their men would have had to row or sail themselves out to the fishing grounds and the women would stay at home, constantly occupied with the business of mending nets or repairing equipment and clothing, unless they were out selling the fish their men had caught — in this case, a meagre basket of shrimps. The work went on throughout the year and there were few days when the people who lived from the sea did not need to be protected against the weather. These women wore hand-knitted head scarves but their woven shawls probably came from factories in England.*

There are no fishwives left in Tenby today and the fishing boats are more likely to be used for pleasure trips round St Catherine's Island or out to Caldy Island where the monks make liqueurs and pomanders to sell to the summer visitors.

Fishermen, Sheringham, Norfolk, 1893 (right). *The Sheringham fishermen were evidently a tough, independent-minded lot, judging by the different ways they are wearing their sou'westers. They needed to be for their fishing grounds in the North Sea, though rich in cod, mackerel and herrings, were dangerous.*

There are two Sheringhams: one above the cliff and one along the shore where the fishermen lived. Six years before this photograph was taken a railway branch line had reached Sheringham, bringing with it both summer visitors and inevitable change. Houses for holidaymakers sprang up round the old fishing village and Sheringham became a 'resort'.

The fishermen's cottages are still there, though a new lifeboat, now launched into the sea by a tractor, has replaced the old sail-powered one which is preserved in its original shed. There is still a fishing fleet in Sheringham devoted to catching the lobsters, whelks and crabs that abound along the Norfolk coast.

The mill, Hornchurch, Essex, 1909 (above). *This splendid wooden mill at Hornchurch was in the midst of the countryside east of London in 1909, an area later to become well-known when the Ford Motor Company installed its factory at Dagenham. In this picture, the local baker, who has arrived to collect his sacks of flour, seems to be about to approach the schoolboys who are collecting blackberries - perhaps to find out if they are playing truant? Unfortunately, the mill was burned to the ground in the 1930s, at a time when the large machine mills were well into their own.*

Welsh weaving, 1903 (right, bottom). *The phrase 'cottage industry' may have a pleasant romantic ring to it but most work in country people's cottages was a form of sweated labour. The machinery necessary for the work was installed by an industrial entrepreneur who would pay for the items produced deducting the amount owed to him for the use or purchase of the machine. As piece-work was very poorly paid, the cottager had to keep going far into the night, working by candlelight, in order to produce enough goods to earn a living.*

Hop picking, Tonbridge, Kent, 1890s (below). *The gentleman in the traditional farm labourer's smock looks more like the owner of the hops than an itinerant picker. Hops, an essential ingredient in making beer, are harvested in late summer. Once collected they are taken* *to the oast houses whose cylindrical brick towers topped by conical roofs are a familiar sight in south-east England. Here the hops are dried before being used in brewing beer.*

Until recently hop-picking provided townsfolk with a few days working holiday in the countryside.

America in the 1870s and which would, in the first decades of the 20th century, be calling more and more girls away from jobs as servants or shop assistants into office employment.

Early in Victoria's reign, young country boys fared little better than their sisters; most of them were unable to read or write and could only find unskilled work in the towns. A few were employed in stables and there was also a certain amount of work in the big food markets for young boys from the country, but most of them ended up in menial jobs in factories where they worked long hours for little pay.

Working conditions for children

Despite an awakening social conscience about conditions of work, especially in the mines and textile industries where children worked long hours in appalling circumstances, the few regulations that existed were not enforced, even in the mid-century. Many young people between the ages of five and fifteen were virtually slaves, lowered into mines where they spent all day operating ventilator fans or keeping rats away from the men's dinner, or in the potteries where they were engaged to fetch and carry in potters' stove rooms in temperatures seldom less than 120F.

Other children were used by an army of itinerant workers who were outside the reach of legislation: chimney sweeps, for instance, who employed small boys to climb inside chimney flues, a form of work described in terrible detail by Charles Kingsley in *The Water Babies*. Others worked in the sweat shops which had grown up as a kind of urban cottage industry making articles of clothing during a 12-to 14-hour day. It was not until the Factory Act of 1874 that the minimum working age was set at nine years and a 10-hour day introduced.

The ways of making a pittance were as many as human ingenuity could devise. There were, for

Strawberry picking, Swanwick, Hampshire, 1890 (above) *Today travellers on the M27 motorway are hardly aware of the village of Swanwick which lies between Southampton and Portsmouth, but at the turn of the century this was a halt for the 'strawberry train' which arrived with fruit-pickers to harvest the crop of strawberries.*

In the 19th century harvest time still had a meaning for townspeople, perhaps because many of them could remember the years when they or their parents lived in the country. At any rate thousands of them would become part-time harvesters of fruit and hops in the autumn and this would be an occasion for communal enjoyment as well as earning extra money. Today strawberry picking is still a day out but to more hedonistic ends.

Hill farming, Cumbria, 1900. *In the hilly country of what was once Westmoreland, and is now part of Cumbria, life was hard, tugging a living from the thin soil. In this picture a farmer is leading his horse down to lower ground with a crop gathered from the upper slopes of the valley sides. Today, the farmer would use a tractor or more probably graze sheep. If he possesses any horses at all they are probably hired for trekking to the tourists who throng the Lake District every summer. The use of sledges in this manner is now only employed as a novelty.*

Tourism is a more profitable livelihood than agriculture in this beautiful but rugged land and many farmers have given up the struggle. Their land has, however, been preserved from exploitation by the National Trust who own vast acres of the magnificent landscape and who ensure that the millions of visitors do not destroy it.

example, men and their boys who collected the horse dung that littered the streets of every town and village; others stood at crossings to sweep them clean of the horse manure and sand was strewn to ease the passage of horse-drawn vehicles so that pedestrians would not dirty their shoes; others combed the sewers for whatever they could find, and some even gathered up dogs' droppings for sale to the tanneries. Crime, too, offered all kinds of opportunities for young people, as was so vividly described by Dickens in *Oliver Twist*.

The survivors

Those who survived the hard apprenticeship of life in an industrial city set up home in miserable tenements little better than the dilapidated country cottages from which they had come; those who did not, sank in the social mire, sleeping in doss houses or becoming resigned to the workhouse until disease ended their misery. Charles Booth, founder of the Booth steamship line and one of those public-spirited men who did much to change the pattern of city life for the poor, described them as the lowest class for whom 'the common lodging house caters for their necessities and the public house for their superfluities. Their ultimate standard of life is almost savage, both in its simplicity and in its excess'.

They had better prospects to strive for and by learning new trades managed to pull themselves up into a better level of life. Three-quarters of the way through the 19th century it was already evident that the tide had changed and that the working people in industrial areas were living a better life than they had done in the country. The men who had learned new trades, and now called artisans rather than craftsmen, were the stone masons and carpenters for whom there was an increasing amount of work in the expanding cities, the iron founders, the printers, and the workers in all branches of industry in which specialized skills became necessary as the industrial machinery grew more sophisticated. There were also more jobs in service industries, the railways offering some quarter of a million jobs by the turn of the century and the food industry well over half a million.

This increase in the number of men in industrial employment, most of whom were also now better educated, brought about a gradual change in the relationship between employers and workers and strengthened the will of the workers to demand better working conditions. Improvements took place in industrial life as the bargaining power of unions grew, though some also came from far-sighted employers like William Lever, Lord Leverhulme, who founded Port Sunlight where he provided his workers with good housing and improved working conditions.

In parallel to developments on the labour front, there were considerable changes in the work offered in the service trades. Shopkeepers, plumbers, gas fitters, electricians, and many others were in demand as more and more terraces of houses were added haphazardly to the urban sprawl. Such trades, both retail and service, were seen as being a cut above the manual workers in the social scale but below middle-class, white-collar workers.

Influence of the middle class

During the Victorian age the middle class became the most important influence on national life; they were a class which believed with Samuel Smiles that everyone could succeed by their individual efforts to improve in every sphere of human activity. Life was a competition, which was in every aspect of social life, work, play, the house one lived in, one's friends, social behaviour, dress and even the kind of pets one possessed.

It was important to start up the success ladder in the right kind of way. The working life of the

Knife sharpener, c.1900 (above). *In the days before retail shops selling every kind of merchandise and service lined the High Streets, there was a considerable amount of trading by individual peddlars and hawkers, and most household services could be attended to by itinerant craftsmen who could mend chairs, kitchen equipment, and even sharpen cutlery. The knife-grinder like the one in this picture who adopted the respectable bowler hat and suit of the middle classes was often a regular visitor and most households would allow him to clean and sharpen all their knives and scissors every week or two.*

All street peddlars were uneducated and came from the most poverty-stricken homes, or no homes at all. Their trades were usually learnt from others like themselves and they were often provided with the initial equipment of their trade by a man who controlled a number of peddlars.

The largest and best organised class of street traders were the costermongers whose leaders came to be distinguished by their fancy clothes which included elaborate ostrich feather hats for the women and pearl button covered suits for the men and were known, as they still are, as pearly kings and queens.

The Matchseller, 1890s (below). *This barefoot matchseller was one of an army of itinerant workers who earned their money in the cities of Britain as touts, hawkers and entertainers. Matchsellers were nearly always destitute young boys, many of them Irish, with no schooling and almost totally in ignorance of the three great principles which inspired – for good or ill – middle class Victorian society: God, Queen and Country.*

Among a nation of pipe and cigar smokers, matches were always in demand and manufacturers vied with each other in producing eye-catching covers for them which are now sort after by collectors.

Draymen Reading, Berkshire, 1940s (above). *Breweries have always provided plenty of work and in the days before motor transport employed thousands of country people who knew about the care and handling of horses from their work on the land. Horse-drawn drays were used for delivering beer until recent times, though the last ones are on the road for publicity purposes rather than for practicality. The horses drawing the drays were fine specimens of shire horses and the drays themselves were examples of excellent craftsmanship with hand-carved wooden sides and painted name boards at the front and back. The beer drays shown here belonged to H & G Simonds, Brewers of Reading, later a part of the Courage group.*

The brewing industry was a source of income to many people in the Victorian age. Opening hours were long and consumption of alcohol in its various forms was astronomical, particularly among the working class.

Shopping

In the past century, shopping has changed beond all recognition, from an individual social activity in which shopkeeper and customer had an ongoing personal relationship, to an impersonal, mechanised ritual conducted in vast cathedrals of consumerism. In Victorian times each village would have had its local shop where almost all but the most specialized of provisions would have been bought. Periodically the mother or father of the house would travel to the nearest town to buy clothes or other hardware which could not be procured locally. Today supermarkets and latterly vast hypermakets offer a range of merchandise which would have been inconceivable in Victorian times.

The Old Chemist Shop, Knaresborough, North Yorkshire, 1911 (below and right, below). *In the days before proprietary medicines, pharmacists made up most of the doctors' prescriptions and sometimes placebos of their own invention. In this famous old shop in Knaresborough's market square, the pharmacist must have been a busy man, for the visitors to the spa were already inclined towards medicinal treatments for their ailments, real or imaginary. A board outside the shop proclaimed that 'The Ancient Pharmacy' was 'The Oldest Chymists Shop in England Established 1720'.*

Great Bentley, 1900 (right). *Before the days of super markets all villages had a small general store owned by an individual or a husband and wife. This one in Great Bentley on the south east tip of Essex seems to have been run by the couple standing in the doorway. He probably looked after the groceries and provisions and she the millinery and drapery. Orders placed by the local customers would be delivered by the errand boy, but many people would have liked to drop in for a gossip or to discuss the quality of the bacon or cheese. Today, most have been put out of business by easy access to shopping centres such as the one shown on the left.*

middle-class, white-collar worker began with his schooling, then his launching into the world of commerce became a matter of vital importance. Fathers would study – or cultivate if they could – potential employers with the same dedication they would show in looking for a suitable bride for their ambitious offspring.

Young men whose fathers had paid for them to go to a school with a high reputation or even to a university, would have a head start. They would go on to find a place in such professions as the law, medicine, the church or the army. Others, rather less privileged, would enter a bank, an insurance company or some merchant business dealing with overseas trade. Even these were hard to enter. An introduction would have to be acquired through friends who knew someone in a good position in the house of the prospective employer. The young applicant would then have to go for an interview and fill in long forms with such questions as the schools he had attended, names and occupations of his grandparents, the name of the tennis club he belonged to and whether or not he intended soon to be married. The rigorous examination concluded, the young man might be offered employment at the rate of £300 a year.

It was not much, but it was enough for an ambitious youth to set his foot on the first rung of the ladder to a home in Beulah Hill, with a small front garden and a tradesmen's entrance leading to a backdoor where his servant would deal with those who supplied his modest household needs. The young man never aspired to become one of the ruling class himself, but the time might come when perhaps his daughter, if she were pretty and vivacious, might become a 'lady' and when his son, if he had a good head for business, might even become the owner of a large company and consort with the aristocracy.

Since the turn of the century the work of the

Thatching, Tolpuddle, Dorset 1940s (above). *The art of thatching still survives today though the kind of roofing that was common to most country cottages in the Middle Ages can only be afforded by those who are prepared to pay for it. The best thatching material was reed and much of it came from the Fens but the draining of the swampy land for modern agriculture has decreased the reed beds. An alternative to reed was straw but the right kind of straw is difficult to find, for the combine harvester damages the stalks and cuts them to a shorter length than when the harvest was done by hand. This thatched cottage is at Tolpuddle, the place from which the Tolpuddle martyrs were deported to Australia for protesting against poor wages and working conditions.*

Hotel workers, Cheddar, Somerset, 1890s (right). *The freedom to travel which developed during the 19th century brought prosperity to many small country villages, especially if they happened to be near a historic site or beauty spot. Cheddar with its hitherto neglected Gorge became a popular destination and the shops, cafés and hotels provided work for the locals.*

The Cliff Hotel had a considerable staff, including smart maidservants with starched aprons, bootboys and general handymen who carried visitors' luggage from the railway station. The Cliff Hotel also catered for cyclists as we can see by the plaque above the name of the hotel, and no doubt when the motor car and charabanc began to arrive the hotel staff was increased to cope.

middle classes has continued along the lines established in Victorian times, though the boundaries between white-collar workers and tradesmen have become blurred and have even disappeared in the higher reaches of these occupations.

The lives of the skilled, semi-skilled and even unskilled working classes have changed significantly. Conditions of work have improved beyond recognition, thanks in part to the efforts of the trade unions, which, powered by the growing literacy and social awareness of workers and the dependence on their services by complex modern industrial society, negotiated with employers a reduction in working hours, increased pay, and protection from ill-use and unfair dismissal.

At present, the further changes that are taking place may not have as happy an outcome. These are the results of the rapid and extensive progress in automated systems of production, the internationalisation of manufacture and the labour market, and the growing aggressive competitiveness of nations once thought of as simply sources of raw materials.

In the immediate present, however, those who work for a living in Britain can bask in the temperate environment achieved by the labour struggles and technological advances of the past, and prepare optimistically for the opportunities of the Euromarket of the 1990s. □

Model T Ford Factory, Manchester c.1912 (right, above). *The final assembly shop of Henry Ford's new factory in England had not yet reached full assembly line production when this photograph was taken. When the factory was fully set up, some months after this, it was run completely on assembly line principles with standardized components which made for straightforward construction at a time when most of the European motor industry concentrated on more individualistic cars.*

Longbridge, 1930 (right). *By the 1930s, the Austin car was one of Britain's most popular motor cars and its maker, Herbert Austin who designed his first car while working for the Wolseley Sheep Shearing Company, had been knighted. Austin's ambition was to produce a car that was cheap enough for a man who could afford a motorbike. He succeeded with his Austin 7 which put 200,000 more motorists on the road in the 1930s.*

In this photograph, workers are inspecting Austin 10 saloons and convertibles which are ready to leave the factory to join the ever-growing flood of cars that were pouring onto the roads of Britain and which would eventually lead to traffic jams.

Today, not only do we have mechanised production lines, factories which produce machines for transport are themselves produced by machines: computerised robots which, no doubt would have fascinated the mechnically minded likes of Sir Herbert Austin and Henry Ford.

Thames shipyards, 1880s. *There have been shipyards along the Thames since London was founded for the surrounding hills provided all the timber that was needed for the ships, as well as for the scaffolding surrounding the hulls, and the rise and fall of the tide was convenient when the launching day arrived. Most of the ships that served the Tudor navy were built along the Thames and, until the 19th century, shipyards lined the banks as far as Rochester and Chatham. Towards the end of the 19th century, the shipyards were still busy and provided plenty of work for shipbuilders from across the Thames, who were ferried to work on clinker-built rowing boats.*

The quayside at Bideford, Devon, 1893 (right).
*The quay on the river Torridge was once crowded with
the ships of Sir Richard Grenville who had captained The
Revenge in a battle against the Spaniards off the Azores
in 1591. Grenville's merchant ships brought goods from
the new world to the Bideford quaysides which have
continued to handle coastal shipping until the present day.*

*The covered wagons on the quayside are a reminder of
Bideford's American connection, as is the rather basic-
looking Newfoundland Hotel which calls itself a Family
Commercial and Posting House.*

*The town which slopes steeply behind the houses on the
quayside retains the atmosphere of its past with its narrow
streets and the old market which attracts visitors looking
for unusual bric-a-brac.*

Grimsby, Humberside, 1893 (right). *Dirty British coasters with salt-caked smoke stacks which inspired
John Masefield's panegyric to the merchant navy, rubbed
shoulders with schooners and square riggers in Grimsby
docks in 1893.*

*The splendid maritime scene with the tall masts, furled
sails, tarred ropes, buoys and barges is given an exotic
touch by the tower, used to store water for the hydraulic
lock gates, which is a replica of the tower of the town
hall in Siena, Italy; both are still erect and proud reminders
of the importance of commerce in the lives of the communities which erected them.*

*Grimsby was Britain's leading fishing port in the 19th
century but has suffered from the overfishing of the North
Sea that has taken place in the 20th century. In spite of
this, the Fish Market is still the most important in Britain
and an attraction for visitors who visit the neighbourhood.*

Blaenau Ffestiniog, Gwynedd, 1901. *The village of Blaenau Ffestiniog lies at the top of a steep valley scarred by slate quarries. Vast quantities of loose slate are piled on the hillside into which tunnels have been excavated in order to extract the slate. This is the largest slate mine in the world, with 42 miles of tunnels, massive machinery restored to working order, furnished quarrymen's cottages and a museum. Many of these caverns provide fascinating trips for today's visitors, who can ride in trams such as the Victorian slate workers used and examine the primitive tools used in the quarrying and splitting of the slate. The Llechwedd Slate Caverns are a complete 19th century slate mine with lifelike tableaux and the massive 200ft high Cathedral Cave. Also on view are demonstrations of slate splitting.*

The labour intensive methods of quarrying slate led to a decline in the industry at the beginning of this century as more and more houses were roofed with factory produced tiles. The relatively little slate that is quarried today is produced much as it has always been but with more mechanisation. The slate is removed from the quarry side with wedges and wire saws or today more likely by controlled explosives. Blocks are then trimmed with great diamond saws and the slates split off by hand with hammer and wedge.

The slate wilderness of Blaenau Ffestiniog today looks much as it did when Francis Frith took this photograph but the railway no longer carries slate to the port of Porthmadog; instead it is operated by the Ffestiniog Railway Society. In summer the line transports visitors through the wooded slopes that rise from Tremadog Bay towards the mountains of Snowdonia.

Logging, Midhurst, West Sussex, 1898 (right).
Trees were still being cut down by axes in 1898 and the logs cut by hand in a saw-pit, in which one man stood below ground and the other above, drawing the long saw up and down in turn. These tree trunks, being hauled by teams of horses at Midhurst, were extremely heavy and progress along the country lanes to the sawmill was slow. In this lovely picture, taken on the edge of the village, there is no sign of the drivers of the logging teams. It may be that they have popped into one of the cottages for a little light refreshment.

Stoneworks, Corsham, Wiltshire, 1907 (left).
The extensive urbanization which took place in Victorian times and continued throughout the Edwardian period gave plenty of work to quarrymen and craftsmen. Stone was used for all important buildings such as town halls, libraries, museums and other edifices designed to create civic splendour. It was quarried and then transported to stone yards where the master stone masons would cut or carve it into the required shapes. The quarry at Corsham probably obtained some of its stones from Portland, the source of some of the most popular stone in southern England, and also from the Cotswold quarries which produced the honey-coloured stones used in building cottages in northern Wiltshire.

Miner's cage, Frog Lane pit, Bristol, 1905 (left). Underground coal-faces were reached by lifts which were no more than wire cages drawn up and down by a cable and winch. The lifts dropped at high speed through the dark well drilled into the earth. Once below the men walked or sometimes crawled to their work. If the mine was large enough there might be a small railway drawn by pit ponies to carry the coal from the face to the bottom of the mineshaft, otherwise the coal was hauled by man power. Miners' lamps provided illumination and caged birds showed by their reactions when gas was about. In this photograph the miners are going underground to start their shift.

Face-workers, Frog Lane Pit, Bristol, 1905 (below). These face-workers seem unperturbed by their cramped surroundings and the fact that the pit props made of tree trunks are the only safety measure against a collapse of the roof of the coal seam. At the turn of the century conditions had changed little from those of the mid-19th century. Danger and discomfort were hazards most coalminers put up with and some had even worse conditions than those shown in these photographs. Though the wealth of the nation depended on coal, miners were poorly paid and their wages and working conditions began to improve only after the great days of coal were over.

Mells, Somerset, 1890s (below). *Although one associates coal primarily with South Wales and the North of England, there were in fact small coalfields all over Britain. The demand for fuel spurred entrepreneurs to explore for coal even in the predominantly agricultural southern counties. In many rural pits the miners worked only some of their time underground, the rest would be spent working on farms or in other local industries. As time went on, and the mines became deeper, more money had to be invested in the mine and therefore more money had to be made. The miners then became full time, pit communities grew up around the pit head and the owners started to demand more and more work from their employees. In 1880 154 million tons of coal were produced in this country, a staggering amount when one considers that the only method of extraction was by pick and shovel and the sweat of manpower.*

In Mells there was evidently an active rural colliery. The miners have left their bicycles by the lowering gear and trucks are standing by to take the coal away.

Down the pit, c.1890. *Before the passing of Lord Shaftesbury's Mines Act in 1842, men, women and children worked down the coalmines. Children, often under the age of ten, would have the job of working the ventilating fans, looking after the pit ponies and other tasks not requiring great strength. The Act made it illegal to employ females and boys under the age of ten below ground. There was no law, however, to prevent women working long hours at the surface and the colliery lasses, as they were known, were used to rough and dirty work at the mines in the 1890s.*

A soldier of the Empire

In the 1890s the total British Regular Forces comprised 230,000 men. The officers were generally from the gentry and most looked upon their service as a recreation rather than a profession. For the enlisted men who 'had taken the Queen's shilling' life was extremely hard even though many had enlisted to escape the deprivations of civilian life. At this time the Jewel in the Crown of the Empire was India which required 70,000 troops permanently on station to keep order and assist the civilian government.

Most British troops were stationed around the Empire in the last quarter of the 19th century. They were transported by sea which was ruled by a navy of 330 ships sailed by 92,000 sailors. Today's complement of technologically trained soldiers and sailors is a fraction of this number.

Parade at Stoughton Barracks Guildford, 1903 (below). *The Stoughton Barracks which were situated near Guildford in 1903 are no longer there, though the Regular Army still has a headquarters in the town, and there is a large military establishment at Aldershot, west of Guildford. In the year this photograph was taken, although a British Expeditionary Force was sent to Tibet, there was little military activity in the many spheres of British influence around the world.*

Sabre practice, the cavalry barracks, York, 1886 (above). In 1886 the cavalry was still regarded as the peak of soldiering, even though artillery had made the cavalry charge suicidal. In the picture the officers practice sabre drill infront of the barracks which also house their horses.

Training ships, Devonport, 1913 (below). The dismasted men of war at Devonport, used as training schools and workshops, appear not unlike the ships of Nelson's time with their rows of gun decks and broad sterns. The ships of the Royal Navy which were in active service, however, had begun to assume the familiar grey paintwork and superstructures of the modern Navy. Within a year of this photograph, the Navy was in action against the Germans in the South Pacific, at the Falkland Islands, and on the Atlantic seeking out the submarines trying to blockade Britain.

Modern fighting machines (above). In less than 100 years naval ships have gone from vast gun platforms, to sleek, horrendously powerful machines which need never see the target. Just one small modern warship equipped with nuclear missiles has more firepower than all the world's navies at the turn of the century.

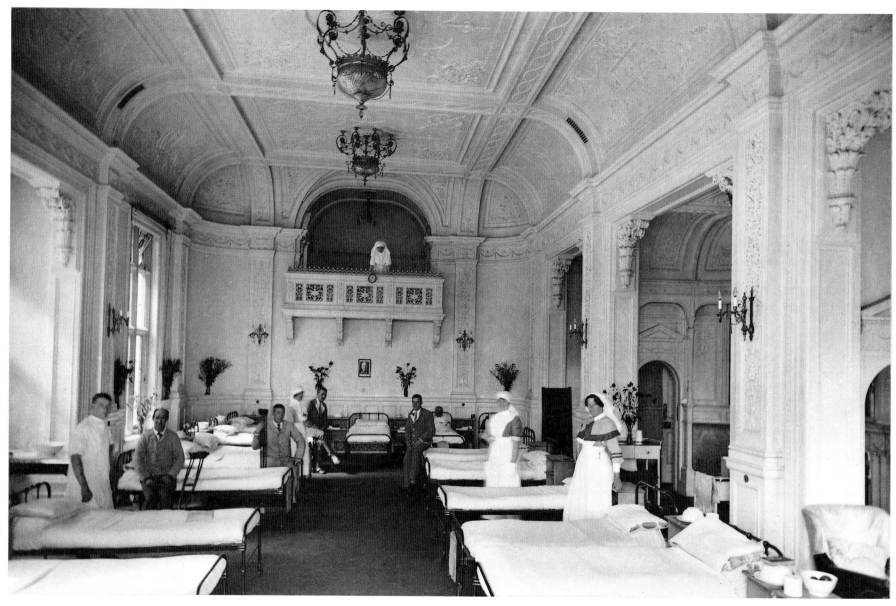

Frensham Hill Military Hospital, The Ballroom Ward, 1917. By the time the Great War broke out, the nursing profession had improved out of all recognition thanks to the pioneering work done by Florence Nightingale during the Crimean War and later. As the casualties rose in the deadly offensives at Ypres, Neuve Chapelle, the Aisne and Loos, private mansions were turned into hospitals and thousands of young women cared for the wounded and the dying. In civilian life health care in the Victorian age was grim. Those who could afford it were cared for in hospitals where medical technology and expertise was very much a hit and miss affair. For the majority of people there was little or no medical care until the National Health Service was set up after the Second World War in 1947.

Postman, Clovelly, Devon, 1936 (left). *The little donkeys of Clovelly, whose main job in life was to transport fishermen's nets from the beach to the village up the cliffside, also learned to carry mail when the motor vans arrived by road at the top of the cliff. The donkeys are still in use today as pack animals on the steep and slippery cobbles that pave Clovelly's only street.*

The Post Office was one of the shining achievements of the Victorian age. Started in 1840 with the introduction of the Penny Post, it soon grew to be one of the biggest government enterprises, owning not only the postal network but also the growing business of electric telegraphy which was taken over in 1860.

Policeman, Romford High Street, 1910 (right). *Sir Robert Peel established the Metropolitan Police Force in 1829 and the new guardians of law and order were promptly christened 'peelers' or 'bobbies'. It was not until 1856 that all county and town authorities were obliged by law to set up local police forces which were supervised by central government inspectors under the control of a Major-General Cartwright. In 1880 the ramshackle local forces were consolidated into 183 regional forces. During Victorian times the 'peelers' were occupied in everything from petty crime to controlling threat to social order, a job thought by many of the upper classes to be the prime reason for the existence of the police in the first place.*

In 1910, the bobby had to be nearly 6 feet tall and his commanding presence, enhanced by the blue helmet, was enough to quell most disturbances. Their job was made easier at that time by the segregation of the different groups of society into different quarters of a city and by the fact that the populace was generally law abiding and united against those who sought to undermine its structure.

The Pursuit of Leisure

Before the 19th century leisure was a haphazard affair; working people took time off from work on Mondays, Wakes weeks, town race meetings or whenever they fancied it. The mass travel introduced by the railways and the demands of factory production lines gradually changed the situation and regular holiday periods were allowed; though without pay. Soon the taste for pleasure became a national appetite which is still unsatisfied today.

Deal Esplanade, Kent, 1899. *The Esplanade at Deal was a popular place for a stroll in one's smartest holiday clothes or to sit and enjoy the sea breeze. The spectacle of the fishermen launching their boats or bringing in the catch and the constant passage of ships squeezing by along the narrow channel between the Goodwin Sands and the coast was a varied and entertaining one to people who could derive pleasure from the simplest things and did not need the complex stimuli required by the modern holiday resort visitor.*

Deal did have other attractions besides those provided by the sea and beach; there was, and still is, a fine example of one of the castles that Henry VIII built when he feared an invasion from Europe along the coasts on which Julius Caesar had landed in 55 BC.

The invasion never arrived and Deal has continued to live a peaceful life, maintaining the tranquillity of yester-year with a pier devoid of funfairs and amusement arcades and the same Esplanade which provided a walk along the sea for its 19th-century visitors.

Charabanc outing to Eastbourne, 1925 (left). *The pneumatic-tyred charabanc made road travel speedier and more comfortable after World War I. It also provided cheaper transport than the train and therefore became popular for excursions. The early charabancs like those in this picture were open, though they had a folding canvas roof which could be pulled forward and attached to the windscreen in case of rain. On some models, plastic windows could be fitted along the sides of the coach. The first recorded charabanc journey was from London to Clacton in 1896, but it was not until the 1920s that they came into general use and undertook journeys from the cities to the seaside resorts.*

Everyone wore a hat for a coach excursion but there was no danger of its being blown off as the average speed rarely exceeded 20 miles per hour.

Teaparty, Northcott Mouth, Cornwall, 1900 (above). *The increasing mobility of the population during the latter years of the 19th century created business opportunities for those who wanted to cater for visitors' needs. Cafes, shops and small hotels thrived in resorts which had previously been impoverished fishing villages. In some places, too small to support establishments that could stay open all the year round or at least during the summer months, the local people set out tables and chairs for the use of visitors. They brought their own food though, as in this picture, but a pot of tea was often provided by the cottagers. This cheerful party at Northcott Mouth seem to have exceeded the numbers that the cottage furniture could contain and a piece of timber on trestles has been set up on one side of the table for the ladies in floral hats.*

The idea that leisure was enjoyable was regarded with suspicion in Victorian times, especially by those who were newly at the top of the social ladder or on their way up. Members of the growing industrial society had only one goal: to work hard in order to surpass their fellow citizens. This was scarcely surprising, for most of them either owned the new sources of wealth or had exchanged rural penury for an urban, industrial life which, though miserable for many, at least held out prospects of escaping the poverty that had been the lot of generations of their ancestors.

For every person who succeeded, there were, of course, thousands who failed to rise above the level of clerks and manual workers, spending 12 to 16 hours a day struggling to earn enough to live a life with few compensations. The better off had always had time for leisurely pursuits and the rural poor had had some satisfaction from such simple pleasures as the joy of the countryside, the seasonal bean feasts, fishing, trapping, some occasional poaching and following the hunts for fox, otter or hare organized by the squirearchy. The urban poor had little to enjoy, and often drowned their misery in gin at a penny a glass: 'drunk for a penny, dead drunk for twopence', as the posters in the Hogarth drawings put it.

The pioneer of leisure travel

It was the plague of alcoholism in cities that inspired the pioneer of leisure travel, Thomas Cook, to launch his excursion and cheap ticket schemes. At the time the Midland Railway opened its line between Leicester and Loughborough, he was secretary of the Leicester Temperance Society. Thomas Cook organized a rail excursion between the two towns, with a visit to a private park, as an alternative to spending time in the gin mills. The trip was an instant success and led to others.

Within a single generation, Thomas Cook was

West Pier Brighton, 1894 (above, and opposite, bottom). *It must have been a chilly day when this picture was taken because most of the strollers along the promenade are wearing warm coats. The cold may also explain why the Pier is deserted, for Brighton's West Pier was very popular with walkers. It had opened in 1866 and stretched 1,115 feet out to sea. But simply promenading about and listening to the band at the pierhead became insufficiently exciting and in 1894, the year this photograph was taken, the Pier was extensively rebuilt to include a new boat-landing stage, a handsome pavilion, shops and kiosks where one could buy a box of sugared almonds or a postcard, and room for many kinds of sideshows and entertainment.*

Today, Brighton's West Pier is a forlorn sight. It is closed and in danger of demolition unless funds can be raised to preserve this relic of the brighter side of Victorian life.

Chain Pier, Brighton, 1870 (opposite, above). *The Chain Pier at Brighton was one of the wonders of its age. It consisted of three sections suspended from four iron-clad piles. It was opened in 1823, a few years after Nash completed the rebuilding of the Pavilion that gave Brighton an exotic atmosphere which set the tone of the resort, made fashionable by the Prince Regent and his friends and followers, but which did not receive the full impact of London visitors until 1841 when the railway arrived. Queen Victoria did not take to Brighton, possibly because she disapproved of her raffish uncle, and sold the Royal Pavilion to the town before setting up her summer residence at Osborne House on the Isle of Wight. The Pavilion is now open to the public.*

The Chain Pier was washed away in 1896 but not before it was immortalized in paintings by Turner and Constable.

established as the undisputed leader of the business of travel throughout the world. His had not been the first leisure excursions: sailing hoy and, later, steamer trips down the Thames from London to Margate and Broadstairs had been made since early in the 19th century, and organized rail trips by Mechanics' Institutes also took place. But it was Cook's persistence and energy that properly established regular excursions to all parts of Britain for working people. At first, these were to the towns and cities, most of which were unknown territory to people who, before the railways, had rarely travelled more than 20 miles from their homes. Even London, which had a more dominant role in the 19th century as a centre of national power and influence than it has today, was as unknown to most of the citizens of Britain as Africa.

When the Great Exhibition opened in London's Hyde Park in 1851 it gave a tremendous impetus to travel and to the business of Thomas Cook, who organised the journey to the capital for some 140,000 workers from the Midlands and the North, about the same number of people as visited Margate each summer. Early in the century Margate was accessible virtually only to Londoners, but by the mid-19th century the railways were putting many more parts of Britain's coast within reach of the working population of the whole country.

Taking the sea air

Visiting the seaside for the benefit of your health was an 18th-century idea, put forward by one Dr Richard Russell in the latter part of the century. He saw the seaside as an alternative to the inland spa, a place to go for one's health, and he recommended the drinking of sea water, laced with port (or milk for teetotallers). Seaside resorts were built, modelled on the spas for the more affluent members of society, Scarborough being among the first. But the real success of the seaside as a holiday place was only assured from the mid-19th century, when the railways began bringing people to Brighton, Blackpool, Mumbles, Southport, Weston-super-Mare and other places round the coast.

Although before the 19th century people had largely preferred to ignore, or even actively detested the wilder aspects of nature, such as mountains and seas, these had now become subjects for wholehearted adoration by those who had fallen under the spell of Romanticism. To sensitive spirits like Charlotte Brontë, who burst into tears at her first sight of the sea at Bridlington, the sea was an overwhelming example of God's works; to others, it was the highway to the Empire on which the sun never set and Britannia ruled its waves.

To ordinary working people, however, the seaside became an increasingly accessible garden of Eden, a place where they could enjoy fresh air and freedom, where they could share the promenades and seafront with the rich and indulge in a sensuality that would have been censured back home. This influx of large numbers of working people set the tone for the popular seaside resorts and they became places devoted to pleasure, their streets and beaches soon full of street vendors, entertainers, fortune tellers, and bathing machines.

The bathing machine was an essential prop in the new theatre of pleasure. It satisfied the twin desire for modesty and for titillation which was typical of Victorian times. It had the same hide-and-seek quality as the long skirts and exposed bosoms of the fashions of the late Victorian and Edwardian period, providing for the ladies the shelter of a cabin from which they emerged on the seaward side and for the gentlemen, the tantalizing glimpse of a bare shoulder, or wet clinging garments spied through telescopes from a cliff top.

Another essential of the seaside scene was the pier, which offered the next best thing to actual immersion in the sea and also an opportunity to

The Beach, Hastings, East Sussex, 1890 (below). *The Hastings fishermen, whose houses and net-drying sheds can be seen at the far end of the beach, had reason to be thankful for the Hastings lifeboatmen for there was no harbour in this busy fishing village exposed to the wind and waves of the English Channel. Hastings developed as a seaside resort in the mid-19th century, with St Leonards, at its western end, being built later as a more select place suitable for well-off, middle-class families. There was, and still is, a great deal to interest visitors for, as well as the fishing village with its boats beached on the sands and its tall wooden towers in which the fishermen's nets were dried, there are extensive caves to visit and a ruined castle at the top of the cliff. Recent additional attractions have been the Fishermen's Museum and Hastings' own 'Bayeux Tapestry' which records the history of the town from the time of William the Conqueror, who landed nearby in 1066, to the 20th century.*

Ventnor, Isle of Wight, 1899 (right). *Ventnor, secluded in its amphitheatre of cliffs, retains a charming Edwardian atmosphere, though today's bathers down on the beach no longer need bathing machines in which to change as they did when this picture was taken. One of the machines is labelled 'for Gentlemen Sundays till 10am', which suggests the custom of allowing men to bathe naked at certain times of the day may have still prevailed at Ventnor in 1899. At nearby Shanklin, a generation earlier, the Reverend Francis Kilvert, whose Diary has, in the recent past, again become popular, had been obliged to don bathing drawers, much to his chagrin, which led him to exclaim that if ladies did not like to see men naked, they should keep away from the sight.*

Because of the restricted space between cliff and sea, Ventnor remains a small and intimate seaside resort and certainly does not encourage motorists to clutter up the narrow promenade.

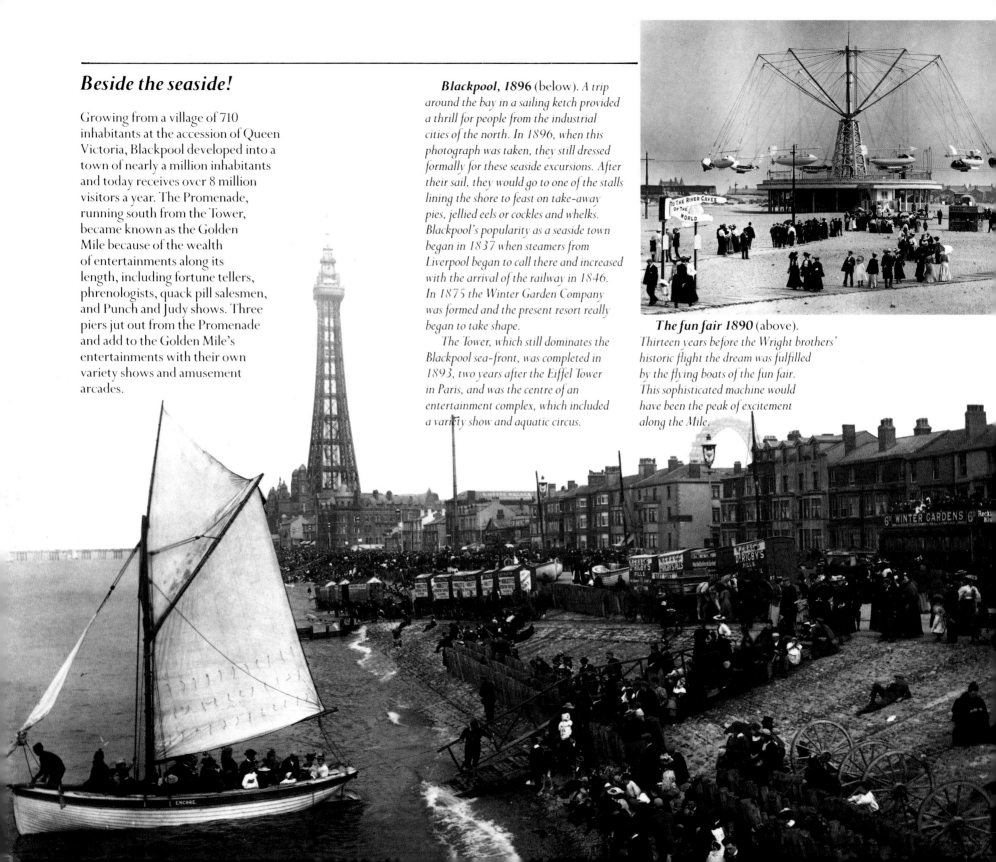

Beside the seaside!

Growing from a village of 710 inhabitants at the accession of Queen Victoria, Blackpool developed into a town of nearly a million inhabitants and today receives over 8 million visitors a year. The Promenade, running south from the Tower, became known as the Golden Mile because of the wealth of entertainments along its length, including fortune tellers, phrenologists, quack pill salesmen, and Punch and Judy shows. Three piers jut out from the Promenade and add to the Golden Mile's entertainments with their own variety shows and amusement arcades.

Blackpool, 1896 (below). *A trip around the bay in a sailing ketch provided a thrill for people from the industrial cities of the north. In 1896, when this photograph was taken, they still dressed formally for these seaside excursions. After their sail, they would go to one of the stalls lining the shore to feast on take-away pies, jellied eels or cockles and whelks. Blackpool's popularity as a seaside town began in 1837 when steamers from Liverpool began to call there and increased with the arrival of the railway in 1846. In 1875 the Winter Garden Company was formed and the present resort really began to take shape.*

The Tower, which still dominates the Blackpool sea-front, was completed in 1893, two years after the Eiffel Tower in Paris, and was the centre of an entertainment complex, which included a variety show and aquatic circus.

The fun fair 1890 (above). *Thirteen years before the Wright brothers' historic flight the dream was fulfilled by the flying boats of the fun fair. This sophisticated machine would have been the peak of excitement along the Mile.*

Blackpool: The Promenade, 1950s. Strolling along the promenade has been a popular activity for visitors to Blackpool from its earliest days. In this picture the modern electric trams that run along the front can be seen; they are the descendants of the first electric trams in Britain, which began to operate in Blackpool in 1885.

Blackpool's Pleasure Beach Illuminations, 1980s. Electricity has played a leading part in Blackpool's success from its earliest years as a seaside resort. The first electric lighting was introduced along the promenade in 1879, the year that Edison invented the incandescent electric light. Electricity also provided the motive power for the famous trams and the fun fair rides at their southern terminus by Victoria Pier. Today, a dazzling tribute is paid to the wonders of electricity, during the Blackpool Illuminations at the end of the summer when the Promenade, its tramcars and the fun fairs that line the route are ablaze with coloured lights.

Tenby, Dyfed, 1890 (below). *Tenby is situated on one of the most dramatic stretches of the Pembrokeshire coast. The little town on its cliff and surrounded by a 13th-century wall, satisfied the Victorians' love of the picturesque; they also found its beach ideal for children as its gentle slope and protective off-shore St Catherine's Island provided safe paddling. For adults who wanted a health-giving dip in the briny, Tenby provided bathing machines manned by stalwart locals who towed them out to sea with the help of horses. There was a fee for this service, though the costs of maintenance were partially covered by selling advertising space on the cabin walls. The machines in the picture seem to have sold all their space to Beechams Pills, who no doubt thought that since the users of the machines were already inclined towards the care of their health, they might be persuaded to believe that the pills, 'worth a guinea a box', would really save on doctors' bills.*

Whitmore Bay, Barry, South Glamorgan, 1900 (right). *Whitmore Bay in South Glamorgan was a good place for picnics at the turn of the century, when eating your lunch in the open was still a novelty. Everyone dressed in their Sunday best for these occasions, the ladies in white blouses and charming frilly hats, which the younger devil-may-care girls on the right of the picture discarded, and the gentlemen in suits and hats or tartan caps.*

The Whitmore Bay beach, whose broad sandy stretch is not shown here, was appreciated by the inhabitants of Barry who had seen their small town grow into an important coaling port and the island, on which Whitmore Bay is situated, joined to the mainland by a causeway and built over. Today, the coaling business has diminished but Barry still flourishes as a port and cargo ships line its quays. The resort has also grown to an extent that the people in the picture would not recognize, for now it has one of the largest fun fairs in Wales, an outdoor sea-water swimming pool and scores of other entertainments.

Rhyl, Clwyd, North Wales, 1914 (right). *The basket-work chairs on the beach at Rhyl protected seaside visitors from the chill winds as they enjoyed the last days of peace before World War I. The popularity of the resort with its fine sands grew during the Victorian period for it was easily accessible by steamer for the increasing numbers of industrial workers penned in the grimy cities of the North. The splendid domed entertainment centre not only served as a venue for concerts and theatrical shows, but was also a sheltered vantage point from which visitors could watch the activity on the beach. In 1914 there was still some 19th-century formality evident on the beach and people tended to dress up, though by now the voluminous bathing dresses of Victorian times had become close-fitting cotton garments.*

Rhyl has continued to grow as a seaside resort throughout the 20th century and now has a gigantic fun fair and holiday camp. One of the resort's enduring attractions is its proximity to Snowdonia and the historic castles of Conwy and Caernarvon.

join a parade whose main purpose was to examine other visitors to the resort, and in particular, for the young people, members of the opposite sex. More open sexuality was very much a part of behaviour at seaside resorts and became a theme of the picture postcards which first made their appearance there.

Character of resorts

A resort's character was very much conditioned by the nature of the towns from which it provided an escape. Blackpool, for instance, which was easily accessible from industrial cities like Manchester and Bradford, became a resort with attractions appropriate to the working class visitors who frequented it. Those who liked to consider themselves middle class tended to go to quieter, more 'genteel' Lytham St Annes or Southport. In the south-east of England, a similar distinction grew up between places like Southend and Felixstowe, and Margate and Broadstairs.

Generally speaking, the popular resorts were more extroverted and noisier; open-air entertainments were plentiful and piers were usually full of amusements like machines labelled 'What the Butler Saw', scenic railways and helter-skelters. More select resorts, on the other hand, set out to be quiet and dignified. To some extent the characteristics which distinguished the resorts in Victorian times are still found in them today.

Though the seaside was the most universally popular destination for the Victorians, and still is for us today, many other places became accessible to more and more people as the 19th century wore on. Most of these provided activities which had always been available to country people but from which the urban population had been excluded simply because their distances had made them difficult of access. Walking and picnicking became motives for excursions to the countryside

Aberystwyth, Dyfed, 1899 (below). *In the 18th century, Aberystwyth attempted to join the ranks of fashionable spas on the strength of its chalybeate spring, but its real popularity as a leisure resort did not arrive until the 19th century when the Marine Terrace was built. Today, Aberystwyth is not only one of Wales' leading west coast resorts but also a university town to which students come from all over the world. Part of the University lies by the sea, not far from the ruins of the medieval Castle. The Castle itself was built on the foundations of an older one by Edmund of Lancaster, brother of Edward I. The major part of the University and the National Library of Wales, which holds over 2 million books, are both to be found on the steep hills overlooking the town.*

The town's appearance has changed little since Victorian times and the sweep of the seafront with its bay windows is very evocative of former times. The Marine Terrace was a place for promenading, and visitors would drive up and down it in their carriages, or stroll along the pavement. Aberystwyth's links with the past provide one of the attractions of the resort for summer visitors in the form of the Rheidol Railway.

Scarborough, North Yorkshire, 1897 and 1950 (right). *Large numbers of visitors did not arrive in Scarborough until 1845, when the railway made Scarborough accessible to everyone. Among the town's attractions were its mineral and sea-water springs, thus combining the attributes of a spa with those of a seaside resort. 'Taking the waters' was, for many, only an excuse for a holiday and for experiencing a lively social life, for which Scarborough catered with its great hotels like the Grand, which dominates the centre of this picture. The Grand, full of every modern convenience, opened in 1867, and is still there today. Among the houses pulled down to make room for it was the boarding house in which Anne Bronte had died of consumption in 1849.*

The smartly dressed people strolling about are out on the obligatory Sunday church parade, a great opportunity to examine other visitors and comment to one's own group on the style, or lack of style, of others. In the 1950s, (right, below) Scarborough was still the place where Yorkshire people went on a Bank Holiday or at the weekend. Although the dress had changed, the need to examine the other visitors seems still to be in vogue!

and prompted the introduction of special trains which set off from the industrial cities to such areas of natural beauty as the Lake District, the Peak District, Snowdonia, the Trossachs, the Yorkshire Dales and the Pennines.

Sporting events

Sporting events which had previously been of a purely local nature began to arouse national interest as forms of leisure entertainment. Football, which had been played since Tudor times but whose rules had never been properly codified, started to take on the character of a national sport. The first football club was founded in Sheffield in 1855. By 1863, when the first meeting to draw up a set of rules was called, there were 11 London clubs, and by 1882, when the F.A. Cup competition was played, there were over 70 clubs in England and Wales. The finals of the competition were played at the Oval on the grounds of the other great popular British sport, cricket, until 1892, when the Surrey Cricket Club became alarmed at the damage caused to the pitch by the 25,000 spectators who turned up for the event. After that year, the finals were played at Crystal Palace. The growth of football to its present-day eminence as a leisure occupation is paralleled by that of county cricket, which had begun in an unregulated manner in the 18th century and become established officially in 1873 with a championship between nine counties.

Though the finals of both football and cricket championships were held in London, the easier mobility throughout the country offered by trains created a growing interest among supporters of local teams who were then able to travel to other towns to cheer on their side. Other team sports like rugby and hockey, also benefited from better and cheaper transport, so did horse-racing, steeplechasing and cockfighting, all of which appealed

to the gambling spirit of the people as much as to their love of sporting contests.

Taste for leisure

Once this taste for leisure began to develop, there was no end to the reasons which could be found for taking excursions. Cities like York evolved elaborate galas which included firework displays and ascents in balloons; London arranged exhibitions and pageants, and events of once purely local interest became national attractions. Among these were traditional customs whose origins had long ago been forgotten but which had become part of the national heritage.

The taste for leisure acquired in the 19th century by the working people to whom the pleasures of the more affluent classes became accessible has continued to grow, and the means to enjoy it has increased. Seaside resorts today cater for every kind of amusement including theatres, concerts, cinemas, ice-rinks, cabarets and museums, as well as sporting championships and leisure facilities from wind-surfing to horse-riding. Inland the range of diversions is increased by such activities as pot-holing, canoeing, rock-climbing and hand-gliding. Today, 'leisure' is a major industry, earning more money than the manufacturing industries whose workers first gave leisure its impetus. □

Rothesay, Isle of Bute, 1897 (right). *These splendid paddle steamers are offering excursions in the Firth of Clyde, where one of the first successful paddle steamers, the* Comet, *made its maiden trip in 1812. Though superseded in the Atlantic crossing by screw-driven ships, paddle steamers continued to provide services along Britain's coasts well into the 20th century and today the excursionist can even take a paddle boat ride down the Thames. From Rothesay, a service to Ayr, Troon and Dunoon on the* Caledonia *operated as late as 1962.*

Burnham-on-Sea, Somerset, 1907 (left). In Victorian times the donkey was an ubiquitous beast of burden, used for carrying loads of all kinds and pulling carts, and many people felt the same sentimental attachment to them as they did to their pets. When the seaside became the most popular destination for family holidays, donkeys found a new role in life giving rides to children, many of whom had never been to the sea before. Here there are more girls than boys preparing for their ride; judging by the expressions on the boys' faces, it seems they have a more competitive attitude to the brief excursion.

Gorleston-on-Sea, Norfolk, 1908 (below). The resort of Gorleston-on-Sea lies to the south of Great Yarmouth at the mouth of the River Yare. Gorleston was the home for a time of John Sell Cotman, the famous water-colour painter of the Norwich School. The tranquillity of the place that inspired Cotman were also the qualities that attracted the Victorian visitors.

Like most of the adults of their period, the children, too, here seem interested in collecting specimens of the sea's natural flora and fauna; one group is gathering seaweed while others appear to be searching for shells and small crabs deposited by the tide on the shore. A certain informality is evident even among the children who have taken off their footwear to paddle. It is a sobering thought that many of these little boys enjoying a day out would probably not have survived the First World War.

The pier that can be seen in the background is the southern extremity of Great Yarmouth, now a large and busy seaside resort with all the hustle and bustle that ice-cream and amusements bring with them. Gorleston is officially part of Great Yarmouth, though it has managed to retain a certain peacefulness as no cars are allowed.

Seaside entertainment

As the Victorian's appetite for leisure grew so the holiday resorts began to provide more entertainment. Resorts began to cater for all the holiday makers tastes as they competed with each other for custom.

There was always something to do, from a stroll along the prom to watching galas, regattas and fairs.

With the bandstand came the pier, then the street performers and Punch and Judy shows, concert parties and fairgrounds. With World War II over up sprang the new Billie Butlin holiday camps with their 'campers' and red-coats.

Today, we demand more sophisticated entertainment with the amusement arcades and leisure centres.

Concert Party, Bridlington, 1906 (below).
Concert parties were performed in the open air when the weather allowed in Edwardian Bridlington. The programme consisted of songs, dances and a bit of tomfoolery. The performers had to work hard to attract and hold the attention of spectators. If they failed, the coins in the pierrot's hat would be few. Though it was a hard life, the seaside concert party gave an opportunity to many entertainers who later became famous on the London stage, including Max Miller and Stanley Holloway.

This kind of spontaneous, ad lib entertainment died out as the seaside crowds increased and life at the resorts became more regulated; perhaps, too, the innocent exuberance of the early years of seaside holidays was replaced by a more blasé attitude. This particular concert party was accompanied by a harpist and a harmonium player

The sands at Swansea, 1910.

The industrial development of Swansea during the heyday of the South Wales coalfields did not detract from the delights of the great sweep of sand in the arc of Swansea Bay. The docks were at the eastern end and at the mouth of the river Tawe, but to the west lay a residential area with spacious parks and sandy beaches. No-one objected to the railway running along the shore for it made the beaches easy to reach as far as the Mumbles, a popular resort on the western headland of Swansea Bay. The Mumbles-Oystermouth railway was the first to carry passengers in Britain, though it was drawn by horses when it began its services in 1807. Entertainments on the beach at Swansea in 1910 included a helterskelter and amusements stall; today the diversions are more sophisticated with a heated swimming pool, theatres, cinemas and numerous sports facilities.

Leisure lands (above). Today many of the people who would have gone to holiday camps in Britain take holidays abroad in countries where the sunshine is more certain. In Britain the holiday centre idea still survives successfully and includes such sophisticated enterprises as the Centre Park where large water leisure areas are under cover in a vast structures with a conditioned atmosphere.

Holiday Camp, Scarborough, 1950s (right).

The establishment of holidays with play for all after World War II revolutionised the business of leisure. The austerity of the post war years when there was still food rationing and a limited foreign currency available for those who wanted to go abroad led to the development of economical home holidays in specially designed camps. Pioneers like Billy Butlin and Fred Pontin provided individual bungalows for visitors to the camps and a busy programme of entertainments which went on from the first cry of 'Wakey, Wakey' until late into the night. Sports, even beauty contests, knobbly knees competitions, amateur nights, conducted walks, swimming galas were popular with people who had become used to community activities during the war years.

Southport, Lancashire, 1913 (left). *Southport was always regarded as a quieter, more genteel resort than Blackpool, designed for quiet strolls along the tree-lined avenues or in the park by the beach. In this picture there is a glimpse of the kind of visitors that Southport encouraged; in the centre, a lady in a bath chair chats with her young companion, two elegantly dressed ladies in long coats walk to an appointment, perhaps at a tea shop. A young man in a sailor suit crosses his legs in boredom and two girls keep an eye open for any handsome young fellows who might pass by.*

Lord Street is still the main thoroughfare of this attractive Lancashire resort and has retained many of the buildings seen in this picture. It is more lively, however, today than it was in Victorian times, with a marine lake, fun fairs, and facilities for every kind of sport. The long pier, built to enable passengers to board boats, which had to anchor further offshore when the beach began to grow wider with sand deposited by the sea, is still there, complete with a railway to carry people to its seaward end.

Dawlish, Devon 1891 (right). *The man in the rowing boat with his salty seaman's cap is no doubt waiting to give someone a sea view of the strange rocks found at Dawlish. Popular fancy has named these the Parson and the Clerk, though it is difficult to see why. Perhaps it is the air of Dawlish that stirs the imagination for Charles Dickens made it the birthplace of Nicholas Nickleby and Jane Austen was particularly fond of the place.*

The inspired inventor and founder of the Great Western Railway was also driven to push his trains along this shore by means of pneumatic propulsion — called the Atmospheric Railway — but this proved to be a failure as the sea water rusted the air-tight joints in the pipes.

Today, Dawlish retains its sedate Victorian look and in summer its beaches are filled with visitors who are inspired to do as little as possible as they sit in their deckchairs or take an occasional dip in the sea under the eyes of the clerical rocks.

Windermere, Cumbria, 1887. *The town of Windermere lies above the lake and spreads down to Bowness, on the water's edge. Before the age of the motor car, visitors to the Lake District arrived by train at Windermere and continued to their destination by horse-drawn vehicles or by steamers, such as the one seen here leaving Bowness pier. Though Windermere's railway station is still in use, most visitors come by car, congesting the streets of all the popular villages, especially Windermere and Bowness which now have large shopping areas, amusements and many restaurants and cafes.*

There has been a good deal of new building at Bowness since this picture was taken but most of it has been discrete and has not spoilt the lakeside. The ferry across the lake from Bowness is now a car ferry, and is very popular because it cuts the driving time considerably to nearby Sawrey and the house of Beatrix Potter, the most visited National Trust property in Britain. During the summer, the queues at the ferry cause long delays.

Mount Snowdon, North Wales, c.1870. *The fashion for climbing mountains that developed during Victorian times was inspired by such British climbers as the Reverend Coolidge, who climbed 1,700 summits in Switzerland, and Whymper whose disastrous attempt on the Matterhorn became the stuff of legends. Snowdon was less arduous than the Swiss mountains and more within the reach of ordinary mortals, so the highest summit in England and Wales became a pilgrimage spot for people who liked a taste of adventure with their leisure. The appeal of Snowdon was heightened by its romantic mythology, for it was here that King Arthur had slain the giant Rhita Fawr. Here, too, Wordsworth had written some of the lines of his Preludes. Most Victorians took a guide to reach the summit and the lazy or disabled rode on ponies. After 1896, they were able to take a train up the mountain. The railway still operates today, taking thousands of people to the summit. Today the shacks have gone (below) and the cairn has crumbled from the scrabbling of millions of pairs of feet.*

Ascot, Gold Cup day, 1902. *The Gold Cup was first run in 1807, and had lost none of its attraction when this photograph was taken in 1902. Run over two and a half miles during the Royal Meeting in June, it is the most important long-distance event of the flat racing season. The weather seems to have been favourable in 1902, tempting the men to wear boaters and panamas and the ladies broad-brimmed, frilly or flowered hats, not quite as outre as those seen at Ascot today, and no less charming. The wealthy punters up in the grandstand are in top hats and are probably enjoying champagne lunches, a habit started by that* bon viveur, *Edward VII who also instituted the Royal Drive up the course, a custom still followed by HM The Queen. Edward VII, who was a keen racegoer, owned Persimmon who won both the Ascot Gold Cup and the Derby.*

The very first day of racing at Ascot took place some 95 years earlier, in 1711, than the first running of the Gold Cup. The Royal connection was there right from this first meeting, with Queen Anne and her Court attending. Each day of Royal Ascot is commenced when the Queen and her guests proceed down the course by carriage. The Members' Enclosure is renamed the Royal Enclosure and all entry is granted by voucher from St James's Palace. In times past divorcees were not allowed in the Royal Enclosure, today, however, all are allowed entry, even children on the Friday.

Royal Ascot is still the most elegant race meeting of the year and provides an opportunity for celebrities of the aristocracy, world of fashion and the media to display themselves in their finest feathers.

Goodwood, West Sussex, c.1905 (left). *King Edward VII seen here with Queen Alexandra in the Royal Box at Goodwood was a forerunner of the monarchs with a keen interest in horses. A bon viveur and gambler Edward when Prince of Wales had many successes on Britain's racecourses. His horses won the Derby, St. Leger, Eclipse Stakes and the Ascot Gold Cup as well as the Grand National. His sporting successes and his urbane public presence made him popular with all classes of society who saw him as a living personification of Imperial Britain. The first meeting at Goodwood was held in 1802, and the first running of the Sussex Stakes was held in 1841. The course is located in some of the most beautiful countryside in southern England, set high on the Sussex Downs, five miles from Chichester.*

Derby Day, Epsom, 1929 (right). *Many of these spectators at the Derby had little hope of seeing the race winner pass the post, but that did not stop them flocking to this great national event just as they do today. Unlike Ascot the Derby was a popular and predominantly male gathering and satisfied the traditional British man's inclinations towards a bit of a drink and a little gambling. As today, it was the Derby which brought out the punters from London. Bets were placed with the bookies who set up their stalls on the edge of the track and promised, like Birchall in this photograph, sure payment. The board showing the runners shows some famous names like Wragg, Beasley and Richards who was knighted and was champion jockey of England 26 times. Little has changed over the last sixty years at Epsom. The predilection for the trilby has gone — to the chagrin of many commentators one suspects — but the course remains largely the same.*

The sporting life

The 19th century was the time when almost all the sports and pastimes we play today developed. Before about 1850 most 'sports' were the country sort of animal baiting, wrestling and fox hunting for the aristocracy. After 1850, with the migration of people into the towns where space and animals to torment were scarce, other sporting pursuits became popular. Football, played in the 18th century between teams of hundreds over a pitch sometimes miles across – it is still played like this once a year in Ashbourne – became formalised into the great sport of the urban working classes. Cricket, a ramshackle sport in the 18th century, developed by the mid-19th century into the game we know today. Tennis had a rather haphazard start: the Wimbledon Championships began in 1877 to raise money for the Croquet Club. Today, the pursuit of leisure has evolved almost as many sports as their are participants.

Tennis tournament Moffat, Scotland, 1880s (left). *The local tennis tournament at Moffat was a serious affair and everyone turned out in their best clothes to watch well-known ladies of the community politely battling it out with*

underarm services. The game which makes

millions for its modern protagonists began its life in 1873 with the unlikely name of Sphairistike on an hourglass-shaped court at Nantclwyd in Wales.

The first championship at Wimbledon in 1877 was, however, on a rectangular court and with, roughly, the rules observed today, though many of the players used the underarm service until the 1880s. Today, Wimbledon (above) is a national institution with millions of followers throughout the world.

Golf, Sandown, Isle of Wight 1927 (right). *Golf, which had been a game for the privileged since the 18th century, when there were no rules or agreement about the length of a course, became a fashionable game for players of both sexes in the period between the Wars. These women were photographed at Sandown, still today one of the Isle of Wight's more popular courses.*

Cricket at Epsom, Surrey c.1900 (below). *Cricket has been an essential sport at British schools since it was adopted by Eton, Harrow, Winchester and Westminster in the 18th century. The adoption of the game by schools produced a large number of expert players and put a stop to the bribery and corruption which was a feature of matches between clubs and villages. In this picture the boys at Epsom College are playing on what looks like games day, with the first team no doubt in the forground. Excellence in sport was as desirable as excellence at work and schoolboys competed fiercely for a place in the team spending hours in the nets.*

A Sunday afternoon in Harrogate, 1906 (above). *One did not have to go to the seaside to see pierrot shows in 1906 for these entertainers also toured the inland spas. Although the fashion for taking the waters had declined at the turn of the century, a town like Harrogate with its fine surrounding countryside and historic sites still attracted a great many visitors.*

Many of the splendid buildings erected when the spa was fashionable have been preserved, notably the Royal Baths and the Royal Pump Room on the site of Harrogate's best known mineral spring, recently reopened as a museum of the spa. The gardens, originally laid out for spa visitors to stroll in, are also carefully maintained. They include the 200 acres of parkland known as The Stray which surrounds the town centre. Today, Harrogate receives more visitors than ever, though few of these come to take the waters which are still available; most come to business conferences or stay in the town in order to explore the magnificent nearby Yorkshire Dales.

The Royal Hall Harrogate, 1907 (right). *When this photograph was taken the Royal Hall was the latest jewel in the crown of the spa town of Harrogate. The Hall represented a high point in turn-of-the-century architecture and reflected the opulence and stability of the British economy at the time. The splendour has been well preserved and today the Hall and its adjacent exhibition complex is a cultural centre, with frequent drama, ballet and concert performances, though in keeping with modern demands, it also serves as a venue for sporting events and business conferences.*

Although the interior of the Hall has been carefully preserved, there have been some minor changes to the outward appearance but it is the sort of entertainment that you are likely to see there that has changed out of all recognition. The organ at the back of the stage is no longer there and the Hall now possesses the latest electronic light and sound equipment, an addition that would amaze and perhaps shock the worthies who attended the Royal Hall's formal occasions 80 years ago.

Punting, Knaresborough, c.1890 (left). *Yorkshire in the 1890s was not all smoky industry and hours of back-breaking work. During the Bank Holidays or on the odd day off at the weekend the young bucks could bring their ladies to punt on the river. Knaresborough, like York, was an oasis in amongst the heavy industry of the region. It had, and still has, a castle and the grammar school was founded there in 1616. The Victorian visitor may even have travelled to the town's 'dropping well' and looked in on St Roberts Cave.*

On the river at Kingston-on-Thames, Surrey, 1896 (left). *By 1896, Kingston-on-Thames was already too popular for the more fastidious boating enthusiasts. The broad waters of the river were crowded with hired rowing boats, most of them filled with the families of the lower middle classes on a Sunday outing. Those who could not afford a rowing boat strolled along the towpath or crowded the terraces of the Sun Hotel. The man in the cart in the centre of this picture had probably conveyed his family to this popular spot, but most people would have arrived by railway from Waterloo station in London and while in Kingston would have walked to Hampton Court Palace or Bushey Park.*

Today, the banks of the Thames at Kingston are crowded with houses, though the centre of the town on the right bank retains its old market square in which stands the coronation stone where, according to tradition, Saxon kings were crowned from the 10th century.

Molesey Lock, Surrey, 1896 (above and left). *At the turn of the century, the River Thames was one of the preserves of the rising middle classes who were expanding into new realms in the pursuit of leisure. The river, like the promenades of the spas and the esplanades of the seaside, was a place where one could see and be seen but it had the added advantage of the privacy provided by one's own motorboat which reflected the style of the owner's home life. In the photograph taken at Molesey Lock in 1896, the splendid motor launch with its shining brass rail has a cabin where a magnificent lunch, brought aboard in baskets, has been served by the servants in their starched aprons and bonnets. The more adventurous ladies and gentlemen have retired to the upper deck to enjoy the passing scene and to examine fellow river travellers with calculating glances. The motor launch ahead evidently belongs to a humbler excursionist.*

Yachting at Bowness, Cumbria 1897 (below). *The expanse of Windermere near Bowness is a favourite one for amateur yachtsmen who take advantage of the breezes that sweep up the lake from the south. Those who have never tried the sport can take lessons at two schools for outdoor activities at the southern end of the lake and the more advanced can take part in races not unlike the one going on when this photograph was taken 90 years ago.*

Today, Windermere is the most popular and easily accessible of all the English lakes and the only one with a railway station so Bowness, which is down by the lakeside is usually crowded and has large numbers of hotels, cafes and shops. Near Sawrey is the home of Benjamin Bunny, Jemima Puddleduck, Jeremy Fisher and other creatures invented by Beatrix Potter whose small cottage is still very much on the tourist route.

Box Hill, Surrey 1891 (right). *When the Bank Holiday Act of 1871 allowed six days a year of obligatory leisure for working people, everyone rushed to take advantage of the free time. Working people made up picnic parties with their neighbours, railway companies offered special fares, entrepreneurs set up fairs and galas and the whole country was alive with people on the move and having a good time.*

In this photograph they are at Box Hill in Surrey all clad in their Sunday best for a stroll through the woods to the edge of the hill on the North Downs from which they could look down on the rolling landscape of Surrey. The Victorians, ever on the look out for a business opportunity, were quick to set up stalls among the trees where the excursionists could take tea or other refreshments in preparation for the journey home, no doubt on the local charabanc.

Getting About

The arrival of the railways made it possible for everyone to travel and the railways and their agents made sure that they did. When the internal combustion engine was invented the freedom to travel expanded further. The rich sped about the country in their 20 miles per hour automobiles and the poor in open charabancs. Thousands of others took to the road on bicycles. The crowds on the British roads and at resorts impelled some to get away from it all by aeroplane to places which today have become as crowded as resorts at home.

York Station, 1909. *Fast Intercity 125 trains now pull smoothly into York, but the magnificent 19th-century station retains much of its Victorian atmosphere. The splendid span of roof is cleaner than when steam engines poured their sooty smoke on to the glass panels and the platforms are lit by electricity instead of gas, as in the days when the companies using York Station were the Midland and Great Northern Railways.*

The modern traveller looking at this photograph must be impressed by the large number of porters available in 1909 to help passengers with their luggage, which appears to include, on the hand-cart on the right, a basket of racing pigeons ready for despatching for a race against other pigeon fanciers' birds.

Today, York is still a busy railway centre and the site of the National Railway Museum where locomotives and rolling stock of the great days of railway travel are carefully preserved.

In our mobile age it is difficult to imagine a time when getting about in Britain was so difficult and so expensive that few people even contemplated it. In the first half of the 19th century most people rarely moved from their birthplace. An early sign that change was on the way came in 1839 with the publication of George Bradshaw's *Railway Timetable and Assistant to Railway Travel*. This was a very slim volume but it showed that a growing number of people needed information about the movements of trains on the rapidly, expanding railway systems.

The prospects for railway development had attracted entrepreneurs, ushering in a period of euphoria during which railways became an investor's dream. But this soon turned into a nightmare when too many companies launched themselves into the business and began to fight for a market that was not large enough to sustain them all. Bankruptcies followed quickly and the larger and more daring entrepreneurs snatched up the small, failed companies, merging them into bigger ones. One of those entrepreneurs was George Hudson, of York, who came to be known as the Railway King until he lost his throne in 1849 in a crash that ruined him and brought him into the criminal courts for fraud.

In spite of the financial chaos of the companies, the trains attracted passengers in ever-increasing numbers. When Queen Victoria went to Windsor by train in 1842, the distrust of the nation in the newfangled form of transport was laid to rest. Trains continued to be unpunctual, to be derailed and to be dirty and uncomfortable but they became the best way to travel. The rich often had their own railway carriages, the well-off travelled first class in well-upholstered compartments with curtains and mirrors, the middle class travelled second class in similar but less opulent comfort, and the poor were squeezed into carriages with hard

St Pancras Station, London, 1868 (below). *When this photograph was taken Sir Gilbert Scott had just completed the staggering Gothic revival building of St Pancras Station and Hotel, one of the wonders of the London skyline, and now preserved for posterity.*

The monumental station was the terminus of the Midland Railway Company who evidently set out to upstage the severe, avant-garde Great Northern Line station built by Cubbit in 1852 at King's Cross.

The interior of the station seen here was the work of W. H. Barlow. The rails ran on a huge steel deck, below which were cellars where beer brought by the Midland from breweries in Burton-on-Trent was stored. The roof span was the largest in the world at the time. The carriages of the period were simple, consisting of compartments with doors at each side but no connecting corridor.

Cranleigh Station, Surrey, 1908 (right). *Cranleigh Station, on what in 1908 was the Southern Railway line to the South Coast, was typical of the small halts serving rural communities in Britain. Many of them still survive, though not all as railway stations, and their solid brick houses comprising ticket halls, waiting rooms in which coal fires glowed in the winter time, and the station master's home still charm us with their homely, personal atmosphere.*

In 1908 the station master and his men had a fierce pride in their own station and a great deal of spare time was spent in keeping it spick-and-span. As we can see here the platform was spotlessly clean, whitewashed stones marked the flower beds and plants were trained up the walls of the outer buildings much as if they were their own country cottages.

Barmouth, Gwynedd, North Wales, 1896 (left). *The railway running up the west coast of Wales brought visitors to Barmouth across the bridge which carried the steam train across the Mawddach Estuary. The appeal of this 19th-century resort lay in its superb scenery which William Wordsworth had described during his visit in 1824 as sublime. Later visitors were as much attracted by the two miles of sand as by the view of Cader Idris across the Estuary. Some of them, however, inspired by the feats of British mountaineers in the Alps, set out to climb the Welsh mountain named after the great warrior Idris who was killed fighting the Saxon invaders from the east. The railway ran, and still runs through the town of Barmouth between the houses and beach, an arrangement which in the days when railways were regarded with pride and wonder did not seem to detract from the town's attractiveness. The bridge across the estuary is 800 metres long and has a pedestrian path which allows visitors to cross and at the same time to enjoy an unusual view of estuary and mountains.*

Newcastle Station, Tyne and Wear, 1950s (right). *After 1921 the multiplicity of railways that had been launched by entrepreneurs at the time of the railway book of the 1880s had been much reduced and an Act of Parliament rationalized the remaining companies into four regions: the Great Western, Southern, London Midland Scottish, and London North Eastern. The latter served Newcastle whose railway terminus is seen in this picture. Through the busy station passed incoming and outgoing passenger traffic and the goods from inland industrial cities destined for the ships at the Newcastle quaysides.*

Great Western Express, Corsham, 1906 (above). *At the turn of the century the railways were in their heyday and provided comfortable transport in three classes of coach to all parts of Britain. The long distance trains with their massive engines were particularly romantic with their long plumes of smoke trailing behind them as they thundered across the countryside. In order to shorten the journey the trains would run non-stop over long distances, filling their water tanks en route from troughs laid at certain places between the tracks. Those who could afford it would make use of the restaurant car where meals were immaculately served.*

Today, (right) *we have InterCity trains which rush us from one part of the country to another often less quickly than the old steam expresses.*

wooden seats and open to the smoke, soot and cinders from the engine.

Many poorer travellers were induced to travel on the railways by special low price fares offered by agents such as Thomas Cook who began to run excursions.

Effect of railway travel

The effect of railway travel on the people of Britain was enlightening and far-reaching; many people could now see their nation for the first time, becoming aware of it as one country. The beauty of different regions, the squalor of the industrial towns, a sense of national history and the inequality of society began, slowly at first and later gathering momentum, to breed new ideas in people's minds.

The railways brought their own physical changes to the countryside, cutting swathes through hills, building enormous bridges and viaducts, and tunnelling through mountains. Small stations and large termini were built, leaving for posterity physical and architectural monuments to their illustrious heyday. Stations in the big cities were particularly impressive, expressing the solidity and confidence of the railway system and the extent of its power. Many of these still remain: the great Gothic pile of St Pancras station; the severe facade of King's Cross; the Renaissance classicism of Newcastle-upon-Tyne, Brighton and York. Others have gone, including Euston, with its triumphal arch, which was swept away when the station was rebuilt in a modern style in the 1960s.

After about 1870, a new dimension was given to the railways when people began moving away from crowded city centres to the fringes which came to be known as the suburbs. This suburban expansion was most noticeable in London: the city, whose diameter had been four miles, suddenly doubled in size, growing urban tentacles that penetrated far into the country. Encouraging the trend which gained them a captive army of commuters, the railways offered special fares and themselves indulged in property development. By the end of the 19th century the railways were moving more commuters than all the other forms of inner city transport put together.

The railway companies also aimed to take over the freight transport business from the canals which had served the industrial towns since the early days of the Industrial Revolution. The canal systems began to unite in their fight for survival – the Grand Junction, Regent and several other canals becoming the Grand Union system, for instance and the Manchester Ship Canal opened in 1894, bringing cargo steamers into the centre of industrial Manchester, but the canal system in the long run did not stand a chance against the railways. Today, a revival of interest in Britain's canals is largely for the leisure business.

No one at the end of the 19th century could have imagined that the railway system could ever be replaced, but the internal combustion engine, hissing and spluttering in its birth cries, was already on its way.

The bicycle craze

Before motor cars became accessible to all, however, a form of individual transport appeared that was truly democratic and quickly became a national craze in 1894. This was the pneumatic tyred safety bicycle, a machine far superior to the boneshakers and penny-farthings that had preceded it. With the bicycle, everyone gained the freedom to travel wherever they wanted and to feel that they were the equal of all other 'devotees of the wheel', as contemporary newspapers called cyclists. Moreover, the cost of travel, once the bicycle was paid for, was virtually nothing. In the years following the introduction of the bicycle the roads of Britain were filled with cyclists from all levels of society.

The Snowdon Railway, Llanberis, Gwynedd, 1896 (above). *Opened in April 1897, the Mount Snowdon railway climbs the 4.5 miles to the summit. It is the only British railway to use the Swiss Abt track of two parallel rails with staggered teeth.*

The railway greatly increased the number of visitors to the summit and ended the era when to have reached the top was a rare achievement.

Funicular railway, Bridgnorth, Shropshire, 1898 (left). *Bridgnorth, on the River Severn, is a town in two sections: on the right bank of the river is the High Town and on the left, Low Town. The two are connected by this cliff funicular railway whose track is cut into the rock at a gradient of 2 in 3. Funiculars were much in vogue during the latter part of the 19th century, perhaps because of public awareness of the many funiculars in Switzerland, the leading holiday destination for British people at the time. There are also several flights of steps between the two parts of Bridgnorth but most people prefer to walk down these and take the funicular up.*

Crossing the Channel, Dover, 1901. *Travellers for the Continent usually boarded the cross-Channel paddleboats at the Admiralty Pier in 1901 having been brought there by Southern Railway whose trains ran along the Pier. Though by the turn of the century continental travel attracted more and more of the middle classes, numbers involved were still low and the simple port facilities seen in this photograph were adequate. In the post World War II period, Dover harbour has become one of the busiest ports in Britain with rows and rows of motorcars and articulated lorries always parked on the extended quaysides waiting for the car ferries.*

When the Channel Tunnel is completed in the 1990s, these numbers may diminish as motorists and lorry drivers take their cars to France under the sea instead of over it.

Canals and waterways

The great days of canals can be said to run between the 1760s and the end of the 1820s when the Liverpool to Manchester railway was opened. The first truely commercial waterway was the Duke of Bridgewater's canal which ran between the coal fields of Worsey to Manchester. It was built by James Brindley – who also masterminded the Trent and Mersey canal – a millwright from Staffordshire who, although lacking a formal education, was a brilliant practical engineer. When it opened in 1761 it halved the cost of coal transport between these points. By 1830 there were over 4,000 miles of navigable waterways, but their hayday was over. Hard on their heels was the transport of the future: the railways, which were faster and more economical began to grow and take trade from the waterways, until by the 1870s the canal system was almost closed down. Today, we look at the canal system as an asset for recreation, and to be conserved for its unique natural beauty, although a few boats still ply the waters commercially.

The lock and bridge, Chertsey, Surrey, 1890 (below). *The River Thames flowed quietly through rural Chertsey in 1890 and the even-arched bridge carried only horse-drawn traffic. The canal was entered through the hand-operated locks and provided a waterway to industrial towns in the Midlands, as well as a quiet stretch of water for sailing boats like the one the boys in the picture have rigged in the style of a Thames barge.*

Five Rise Locks, Bingley, West Yorkshire, 1894 (above and right, above). *The five-rise locks on the Leeds to Liverpool Canal at Bingley was an engineering wonder of the age when Britain's industrial goods were transported by waterway. It raised canal traffic between Leeds and Liverpool by 100 feet in order to negotiate the Aire gap through the Pennines. Barges loaded with coal or manufactured goods rarely pass through this canal staircase nowadays, and the marvels of the locks are now enjoyed by the narrow boats of leisure travellers and the walkers along the towpath.*

The Grand Union Canal, Kings Langley, Buckinghamshire, 1950s (below). The Grand Union Canal passes through Kings Langley on its route between London and the Midlands. When this photograph was taken it was still a busy waterway used for the transport of raw materials and manufactured goods on the long narrow boats specially designed for canal work. The mill in the background, like many other industrial buildings, was situated on the Canal and provided immediate access to a vast and economical transportation system. In the early days of canals, the barges were drawn by horses that walked along the tow path but later motorized barges made the horse unnecessary and the tow paths became paths for walkers. Today, the canals are rarely used for commercial transportation but continue to serve a purpose as leisure waterways while the long boats fitted out with cabins provide one of the pleasantest and most leisurely ways in which to enjoy the English countryside.

Aristocratic ladies and lordly gentlemen passed clerks, office workers and servant girls cycling along the streets of London to gather at Hyde Park or Battersea Park for their Sunday outing.

The fashion was short-lived among the better classes who perhaps realized that mingling in this way with the lower orders was not appropriate to their station. Anyway, by then there were motor cars to be purchased.

But the rest of society glorified in the new freedom offered by the bicycle, especially women, even though they were regarded by at least one cycling magazine as unfit for feats of speed and endurance and suited only to ladylike pedalling through the park. To which women replied in effect that if they could rid themselves of their long skirts they would be capable of everything. They tried bloomers and 'rational dress' and by the 1930s were cycling about the countryside in brief shorts, celebrating the emancipation the bicycle had helped them to win.

By this time, the heyday of the bicycle was coming to an end as cheap motorcycles became available to all.

Early motor cars

In its early years, the motor car was more a status symbol than a practical vehicle, as was evident from the elaborate design, leather upholstery and brass fittings of such models as the Panhard tourer of 1903 and the Austin limousine of 1908, an early example of a half-closed-in car which was followed by the fully enclosed Renault of 1914 in which the driver was also protected by roof and windows.

Though the enclosed saloon car had come to stay, in the inter-war years the fashion for open cars with hoods continued, perhaps because they projected a dashing air suitable to the liberated, better-off bright young things of the period. Even at that time getting about by car was something

A tricycle, Walton-on-Thames, Surrey, 1893 (left). *Walton-on-Thames was a sleepy sort of place in 1893 with small, two-storey houses and very little traffic. No one in the rural village then could have dreamt that their quiet haven would become a very busy and prosperous part of London's commuter land. A harbinger of things to come was the metal three-wheel bicycle parked by the kerbside which, though regarded as an oddity, was the first of an avalanche of chain-driven vehicles which would gradually displace the horse. This particular model was designed with a front seat on which a lady passenger might sit in comfort in her long and voluminous skirt.*

Cycling down Oyster Lane, Headley 1906 (left). *By the turn of the century bicycle riding by women had become acceptable. Most of them however eschewed the daring pantaloons devised by the American emancipator Amelia Bloomer and wore long skirts. The design of a bicycle without a crossbar made it possible for women to ride bicycles gracefully and without exposing too much leg. There were, however, the delicacies of Edwardian social etiquette to consider. Should the gentleman ride infront of the ladies or behind? Should the ladies discard their long dresses for a more practical outfit? These were testing questions in another, more punctilious era.*

Though there was still opposition to women on bicycles the fashion for cycling — which as the manufacturers Rudge Whitworth pointed out, was followed by Royalty, the Aristocracy and Society — became universal and the roads were filled with cyclists.

A cyclist's stop-over, The Old Oak Tree Restaurant, Cobham, Surrey, 1911 (above). *The Safety Bicycle with pneumatic tyres, introduced in the 1890s, revolutionized road travel for the individual, for though few could afford a motor car like the open tourer in this picture, the bicycle was within the reach of almost everyone. By 1911 there were over 1.5 million cyclists on the road (and six million by 1926), and they were often members of cycle clubs that travelled in large groups. Cyclists also provided a new market for people like Mr H. Baldock in this photograph, who seems to have renamed part of his establishment, Cyclists Rest, and has persuaded the Cobham Cyclists Club to make his premises their headquarters. Like many small shop owners, Mr Baldock seems to be someting of an opportunist and to have set up a motor and cottage cycle works in which he builds cycles to order.*

only for the affluent; others rode bicycles or motor bikes if they were young men, or went on excursions in motor charabancs.

The motor charabanc had made its debut in European cities where, with its solid rubber tyres and terraced seating, it had been used for sightseeing by the increasing numbers who were taking holidays abroad. In Britain, it became a popular vehicle for the factory outings which more enlightened industrialists were arranging for their staff. Within cities, motor buses and taxicabs replaced the horse-drawn buses and hansom cabs in World War I, and in the post-World War II years drove tram-cars off the streets.

Today, road transport has been taken over by car, coach and articulated lorry. Road deaths may be around 6,000 a year, with 600,000 people injured in accidents, but everyone is free to get about even if it only to get caught up in a traffic jam.

Development of air transport

Of all the innovations in getting about made since Queen Victoria's accession, none has been as momentous as the aeroplane. People first really became aware of the significance of the new flying machines through the exploits of the airmen of the Royal Flying Corps in World War I. After the War they were eager to try the new form of transport themselves. Joy rides in open two-seater aircraft were offered for the first time in 1919; soon after, flights across the Channel and over the battlefields were included in the first air travel brochure, which was issued by Thomas Cook.

There were several British airlines in the early years, among them Handley Page, Air Transport and Travel Ltd, which became De Havilland, and Instone. In 1927 they were merged into Imperial Airways, which became British European Airways and British Overseas Air Corporation after World War II and is now known as British Airways.

Electric Tram, St George Street, Hull, 1903 (left). *By 1905 the population of horses on the roads had reached its peak but other modes of transport were already starting to take over. The electric tramcar ran on rails and took its power from overhead tramlines. The cars were confined to the centre of the road by their rails and so were superseded by the more flexible tramcars. Transport in Hull, however, was still a leisurely affair when this photograph was taken.*

Horse-drawn tram and gig, Leamington, 1892 (left). *Several means of transport common in late Victorian England are visible in this photograph, as they pass the 19th century Leamington Parish church. Though the electric tramcar had been already introduced in Blackpool in 1885 Leamington, which received its 'Royal' accolade in 1838, still had horse-drawn trams in 1892. Behind the tram, moving too swiftly for the camera's lens is a gig, and crossing from the left a Victoria baby carriage from which the infant appears about to fall out! Across the street is a three-wheeled handcart used for deliveries of laundry, groceries and other merchandise.*

Central Station, Newcastle-upon-Tyne, c.1900 (below). *The monumental entrance to the railway station at Newcastle-upon-Tyne was built by John Dobson who, at the time of Gothic revivals, followed a more classical line. The station opened in 1850 and had changed little by the turn of the century or, indeed, even today.*

Though there are no longer hansom cabs waiting for passengers and farm carts and drays have been replaced by thundering articulated lorries and vans, the atmosphere of the street remains the same, with the crown spire of St Nicholas Cathedral still rising above the surrounding houses.

In the years between the Wars, flying as a means of transport was accessible primarily to the affluent; even 'tea flights' over London on Imperial Airways' grand H-class biplanes and trips to Paris were, like motor cars, for the better-off. It was not until after 1955, when the new jet aircraft made many propeller aircrafts obsolete before their time, that the cost of flying came within the reach of the general public.

Airfield construction boomed throughout Britain. Soon most big cities had their own airport, some of which became international as foreign airlines began to use them. They had to grow larger, too, to be able to accommodate new aircraft like the Boeing 747 and to handle its 350 plus passengers. When this giant aircraft first flew in 1969, only 139 years had elapsed since the first passenger train travelled on the Liverpool-Manchester Railway; in this short span of time travel had changed the world. ☐

Horse power meets engine power, Hindhead, Surrey, 1906 (right). *The horse bus bringing visitors to Hindhead from Haslemere and Grayshott must have provided an exceedingly uncomfortable ride on its iron-clad, unsprung wheels, but, no doubt, it was worth it for the opportunity it afforded of visiting the Devil's Punch Bowl. The travellers on the solid-tyred, motorised bus arriving from the right probably had an easier time of it, though, as their charabanc was open, they had to shelter from passing showers under umbrellas which proved no doubt to be extremely unmanageable when the bus gathered speed. It is not inconceivable that the passengers of both vehicles are thinking of alighting and entering the Royal Huts Hotel to restore their flagging energies for the return journey. But first — a photograph.*

Williton, Somerset, 1929 (left). *By 1929, although many Britons owned a motor car, for most, the growing bus service was beginning to provide transport to places not reached by the railway.*

Williton, a small village on the road between Taunton and Minehead, had its supplies of Pratts White Rose motor spirit delivered by a small lorry, here parked by the hotel. The village garage is on the other side of the road, near where a couple are walking on the road as a car overtakes them; as it is 1929, almost certainly it slowed down to avoid splashing them with mud, a courteous gesture inconceivable today.

The road through Williton leads to the coast of North Devon, and has remained almost unchanged as it winds along between Exmoor and the sea, though plans are afoot to widen and strengthen it to cope with summer traffic.

Grassington, North Yorkshire, 1926 (below). *The grey stone houses and cobbled streets of Grassington are the same today as they were in 1926 and even a hundred years earlier. Nothing much changes in this little Pennines village in Upper Wharfedale among some of Britain's wildest and most unspoilt scenery. Even in 1926, however, the village was well served with buses which carried both local people and the walkers who used Grassington as their base for exploring such natural wonders as Great Whernside, the cliff-fringed amphitheatre at Malham Cove and the waterfall at Gordale Scar. In 1926, some people came by car, as they do today, but the one in this picture looks of an earlier vintage than the photograph. In those days motorists kept their cars, which were built to last, for many years, and even became as fond of them as of their pet dogs or their favourite pipe.*

The Smithy and Garage, Merrow, Surrey, 1912 (above) **and 1927** (right). *Merrow is a small village to the east of Guildford and until just before World War I many of its inhabitants lived from farming and its ancillary trades. As can be seen from the photograph above, J. Gould and Son were the local farriers and by the look of the magnificent horseshoe entrance to the smithy he was extremely good at his craft.*

Fifteen years later, things had changed (right)*. The farrier business had closed down as more and more people took to motorized vehicles and bicycles. Mr Gould, who must*

have been an adaptable man, is seen here in 1927 beside his garage with one Shell and one Pratts petrol pump. The splendid-looking car behind the liveried chauffeur is a Renault, one of the first fully enclosed saloon cars to have shaft drive instead of the chain system generally used.

Today the scene has completely changed (right)*. On the site, appropriately enough, is a modern petrol station, but there is no sign of the splendid horseshoe smithy or the houses which surrounded it.*

Hawes, North Yorkshire, 1924 (below). *The Yorkshire Dales that cut across the Pennines have had routes connecting the east and west sides of northern England running across them since time immemorial. In the 19th century they were traversed by poor roads which travellers crossed in stage-coaches and gigs, while goods were carried on drays. It was slow and arduous work, especially in winter when roads were often impassable. On the Wensleydale route Hawes, a sheep marketing town, provided welcome food and shelter for travellers. In 1924 many of these were arriving by motor car and goods were being transported to market by van like the one, which seems to be a T-Model Ford, of J. Marland & Co., Glass & China Factors of Morcambe.*

East Grinstead, West Sussex, 1923 (right). *The attractive High Street at East Grinstead has retained many of its old houses, including the 14th-century Amherst House, the 16th-century Cromwell House and the beautiful Sackville College, once a Jacobean alms-house.*

In 1923 the village, now on the borders of West Sussex and Kent, was a tranquil place with so little traffic that the two gentlemen on the right of the picture could stand and chat on the road. Behind them can be seen the War Memorial and the drinking fountain, both things few villages were without. In most British villages horse-drawn vehicles shared parking space with the motor car until well into the 1930s.

Ingleton, North Yorkshire, 1926 (right). *Ingleton, in 1926, was just becoming popular with the outward-bound folk of the nearby cities of Manchester and Leeds, as a base from which to explore the nearby dales and fells. The Ingleborough Hotel, proudly displaying the AA sign, and the Lancaster Banking Company are evidence that the town was the local commercial centre of an area whose economy was almost entirely based around farming. The car is a Jowett two seater first built in 1923. This one seems to have been modified to the owner's fancy, a common thing to do at the time.*

Farnham, Surrey, 1924 (above). In 1924 Farnham was a quiet country town, though some of its inhabitants were owners of the motor cars which British factories were turning out for the world markets. The bull-nosed Morris Oxford, with the convertible top, was one of the most popular British light cars and competed with Ford, who sold 1,817,891 T-models in 1923.

At that time, no driving test was required and a licence could be bought by anyone at a Post Office. Fortunately, the low speed of cars then made accidents less severe.

Rolls Royce Silver Ghost with chauffeur, 1920s (right). The Rolls Royce Silver Ghost of the 1920s was one of the most beautiful luxury cars ever built. It was in 1922 that Rolls Royce had abandoned their one model policy and launched into a series of new designs, which incorporated a four-speed gearbox and four wheel brakes. The Silver Ghost was launched in 1906 and it is remarkable in an age of technical innovation and change that it was produced with minor modifications until 1925.

The model, photographed by one of Frith's sons, with its wire wheels and gleaming bonnet, has a stylishness that evokes the glamourous period of motoring between the Wars, when the motor car was king of the road.

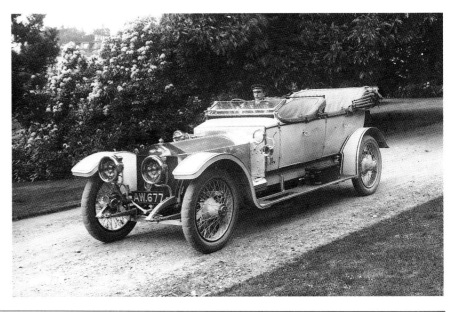

Epsom, Surrey, 1928 (below). *This photograph of Derby Day bears little resemblance to the famous 1858 painting by William Powell Frith. In 1928 the motor car had now ousted the horse-drawn coach at this famous occasion and those with saloon bodies provided a grandstand view over the heads of the tic-tac men whose boards showing the runners and odds can be seen near the rails at Tattenham Corner.*

The classic race, which began in 1780, is the most colourful event of the flat facing season. Today, (right) the course looks much the same, though a new grandstand occupies the place of the one in the photograph and the punters arrive in luxury coaches.

Stoke D'Abernon, Surrey, 1904 (right). *In 1904, the little village of Stoke D'Abernon was a tranquil corner of rural Surrey. In the years since then, the suburban development of nearby Cobham has swallowed its northern half, while to the south runs the new, thundering M25 motorway which orbits London.*

There are no horse-drawn vehicles today, nor the charming tricycle with its wicker chair designed for carrying lady passengers. Some of the old Stoke D'Abernon remains by the River Mole where an old manor house still stands and the church of St Mary's holds the remains of Sir John D'Abernon and his 2 metre long brass effigy, along with many other ancient relics including Roman cornices and a Crusader's chest.

Bideford, Devon, 1924 (left). *The single decker buses trundling along Bideford Quay were a godsend to the people of North Devon who were not well served by the railway system of the inter-war years. The bus services, that ran from village to village along the narrow Devon lanes, made visits to the Bideford market easier and encouraged visits to the glorious North Devon coast, much of which is now in the care of the National Trust. The presence of a large garage on the quayside also suggests that there were plenty of motorists in the area, though not enough to make parking the problem it is today.*

Buxton, Derbyshire, 1914. *The Cat and Fiddle pub at Buxton, home of celebrated breweries, was a popular rendezvous for motorists in 1914. This was still the age of individually owned public houses and the proprietor of this one was Joseph Tomlinson who was licensed to sell British and foreign wines and spirits. Evidently Tomlinson, despite the humble appearance of his premises, had a classy clientele who arrived in their latest open tourers and landaus to the delight of the young girls who seem impressed and amused at the prospective clients. The driver and passenger of the motorcycle and its wickerwork side-car have presumably already entered the premises.*

The Ironclad HMS Hercules, Liverpool, 1890 (above). *Ironclad men of war were introduced into the French navy in 1858 and soon after into the Royal Navy. Hercules was completed in 1868 and at that time was considered the most powerful battleship afloat. She had a long and eventful career during the decades of Pax Britannica and ended her days somewhat ignominiously as an accomodation ship in Portsmouth after World War I. In this photograph, Hercules, with the white ensign on her foremast, is sailing proudly into Liverpool.*

View from Hall Walk, Fowey, Cornwall, 1901 (right). *Though steamships had come into regular use by the last quarter of the 19th century, there were still plenty of square riggers and schooners to be seen around the coasts of Britain. The estuary at Fowey was a sheltered harbour and a trading port for Cornish china clay, as it is still today. Its main attraction for modern visitors is, however, as a holiday resort, for the port has preserved many of its old houses and prevented over development. This view was taken from Hall Walk and shows Bodinnick, a popular place today with amateur sailors.*

Fleetwood, Lancashire, 1908 (left). *The paddle-steamer services along the Lancashire coast helped to open up seaside resorts like Blackpool and Morecombe by providing a means of transport for the industrial workers from Liverpool and the surrounding cities. They were also a means for getting to Scotland before a cross-border railway was established. In fact, they were used for the first Cook's tour to Scotland when the travellers went by steamer to Ardrossan and then on to Glasgow by railway, where they were greeted by a gun salute — such was the novelty of the occasion.*

The sands of Fleetwood, which attracted visitors at the turn of the century, still do so today. The main trade in Fleetwood was, until a very few years ago, the fishing industry. Deep sea trawlers that fish off Greenland would bring in vast catches which would have been frozen on board almost immediately they left the net. The fish would be sold on the dock or bought wholesale by the many large frozen food companies in the area. Today, the fishing fleet is a shadow of the vast flotilla of the 1970s and before.

The Ferry across the Mersey, Liverpool, 1950s (below). *Across the Mersey from Liverpool lies Birkenhead and the Wirral peninsula, a dormitory town area for Liverpool workers, with beach resorts, a golf club and a view of Snowdonia across the Dee estuary. There has always been a good deal of movement across the Mersey between Liverpool and the Wirral and the ferry boats have been kept busy plying between George's Landing stage and Birkenhead. In summer there are also steamer services to the Wirral resorts, North Wales and the Isle of Man.*

During the 1950s and 1960s it was Liverpool which became the centre of a different type of leisure industry. With the explosion of interest in The Beatles, Jerry and the Pacemakers, The Scaffold and all those other Merseyside pop-groups a whole generation allied itself with the area.

Though air travel has reduced the traffic by sea and Liverpool is a far less busy place than it used to be, it is still a major port and cathedral city.

Flight Control, Gatwick, 1937 (below). *The control room equipment consisted of a direct telephone link with Croydon and a teleprinter. Flight clearance and weather reports were obtained from Croydon. The airport of pre-war days still stands, though separated by a dual-carriageway from the new London Gatwick Airport and is a memorial to the vision and persistence of its founders. Today,* (below, right) *is quite a different affair.*

Gatwick, West Sussex, 1933 (left) ***and 1947*** (below). *In 1933, when Croydon was London's airport and flights to the cities of Europe by Imperial Airways, Lufthansa, KLM and Air France had become established, Gatwick was still a part of rural England with a timbered farmhouse surrounded by vegetable gardens and fields. There was a hint of the future, however, in the small hangar which housed the biplanes on which enthusiasts learned to fly with the Home Counties Aircraft Services of Ronald Waters and John Mockford. Their airfield, which was next to the Gatwick racecourse, was occasionally used by aircraft when Croydon was fogbound, but the young enthusiasts were unable to persuade the Air Ministry to develop Gatwick. Discouraged, the pioneers sold out to the Redwing Aircraft Company in 1932.*

By 1937, extensive changes had been made at Gatwick under the energetic leadership of Morris Jackaman and Marcel Desoutter. In 1936, a modern-looking circular terminal building replaced the old hangars and the first scheduled flights to Paris on De havilland 86 aircraft had begun. By 1947 the airfield was again being used for commercial flights following its wartime role. The circular terminal was still there, but was soon to be swept away as the airport expanded. Today, (right) *Gatwick, with its millions of passengers and thousands of flights each year, is something rather different to the peaceful little airfield it started as in the 1930s.*

Imperial Airways. Gangway 1935 (left). *The Handley Page and Short aircraft were the most luxurious of their day. These huge biplanes which flew at only 95 miles per hour were renowned for their quiet engines and excellence of food and service. They served two main Empire routes to South Africa and India, carried only 24 passengers and made overnight stops sometimes in the desert where a special runway with a camp were set up with tents and food, and several European routes with 38 passengers. As the numbers of passengers grew and a demand for much greater speed and lower prices increased, luxurious air travel became only a memory.*

'Air movies', before 1930 (left). *Competition among airlines in the 1930s led to the pursuit of in-flight entertainment. One of the earliest extra services to passengers was the in-flight meal which, on the French Rayon d'Or service, meant a proper sit-down meal with champagne. Cocktail bars were introduced on some aircraft as was radio entertainment, although static often interfered with the transmission. Lantern slide shows were more successful and could be considered as the forerunners of the in-flight movies which is the standard passenger entertainment essential of today.*

The De Havilland DH86A late 1930s (above). *The De Havilland DH 86A was a popular aircraft of the 1930s, carrying up to ten passengers to the Continent. The fare to Paris was four pounds and five shillings single from Gatwick, including first class travel on the train from Victoria Station in London. In 1936, however, two aircraft crashed and this led to an investigation by the Air Ministry which put strict limitations on the aircrafts' operation and grounded some of them altogether. Imperial Airways and other airlines turned to other aircraft such as the Lockheed Electra.*

Index

Photographic Acknowledgements

The photographs in this book are from the Francis Frith Collection, Andover, with the exception of those from the following sources: Allsport, London 214 top, 243; Alton Towers, Alton 135 inset; Heather Angel, Farnham 43 right; Austin Rover, Coventry 179 and inset; Barnaby's Picture Library, London 108 left, 115; Andrew Branson 239 bottom; Britain in View (BTA/ETB), London 27 bottom, 30 bottom, 55 bottom left, 59 bottom right, 139, 155 inset, 167 inset; BBC Hulton Picture Library, London 109, 110, 111 left, 184 left, 185 top, 253 bottom; BSC General Steels, Scunthorpe Works 163; Butlin's Limited, Bognor Regis 207 top right; John Cornwell, Bristol 184 right; Country Life Magazine, London 1, 122 bottom, 123 bottom, 125, 134, 135; Dairy Crest Foods, Surbiton/Chris Pearsall 15; Trevor Dolby 107 top, 110 inset; Ford, South Ockendon 178; Greater London Photograph Library 103 top; Hereford City Library 20; Institute of Agricultural History and Museum of English Rural Life, University of Reading 16, 17 top, 19 top, 21 top, 170 top, 171, 173 right, 177, 185 bottom, 193; The Keystone Collection, London 106 top; The Marquess of Linlithgow 123 top; Museum of London 10; London Transport Museum 108 right; Ian Muggeridge 130 top, 182 top; The National Trust, Llandudno 122 top; Nature Photographers Ltd, Basingstoke/Paul Sterry 127 inset; Northern Ireland Tourist Board, Belfast 74 inset; Octopus Publishing Group: Kubiak & Grange 79 inset, City Engineer's Department, Newcastle upon Tyne 63 bottom, 235 inset, Chris Orlebar 250 bottom right, Raymonds Photographic Agency 55 bottom right, Roger Scruton 47, 67 inset, 223, David Williams 35, Harry Williams 71 inset; The Photo Source, London 11, 19 bottom, 199 top, 227 bottom; Quadrant Picture Library, Sutton/Flight 250 top, 251 top and bottom, 252, 253 top; Jason Smalley, Chorley 42 bottom, 119 bottom, 211 bottom; Spectrum Colour Library, London 159 top right, 170 bottom, 231 top; Frank Spooner Pictures, London 187 top right; Edmund Swinglehurst 22 top, 23 bottom, 51 top right, 83, 150 top, 219 bottom; Judy Todd 7 bottom, 90 bottom, 94 bottom, 103 bottom, 143 bottom, 191 bottom; Zefa Picture Library, London: R. Nicolas 87 bottom, Pfaff 175 top left.

The Publishers wish to acknowledge that some of the pictures contained in this book were researched from the Francis Frith Archive by Mr Bill West.